Cooperative Learning Structures for
Teambuilding

Laurie Kagan, Miguel Kagan and Spencer Kagan

Illustrated by Celso Rodriguez

Kagan
COOPERATIVE LEARNING

Kagan Cooperative Learning.
1160 Calle Cordillera
San Clemente, CA 92673
Books & Materials: (800) WEE CO-OP • (800) 933-2667
Workshops & Consulting: (800) CO-OP LRN • (800) 266-7576

ISBN: 1-879097-41-9

Table of  Contents

- Structures-at-a-Glance .... *III*
- Preface .... *VIII*

• 4S Brainstorming 2
- Role Cards 5
- Team Mascot 7
- On a Deserted Island 9
- One Million Bucks 10
- Team Name Train 11
- The Perfect Weekend 12
- Famous Scientist 13
- School of the Future 13

• Blind Sequencing 14
- Sequence the Store 17
- Sequence the Good News Bear 18
- Sequence the Shapes 19
- Sequence the Fractions 20
- Sequence the Decimals 21
- Sequence the Train 22
- Sequence the Time 23
- Sequence the Holidays 24
- Sequence the Ant Farm 25

• Find-the-Fib 26
- Find-the-Fib Response Cards 29
- Fact-or-Fiction Response Cards 30
- My Life on Screen 31
- Where Have You Been? 32
- I'm Outta Here 33
- Hello, My Name Is 34
- My Favorite Things About School 35
- You're On The Air 36
- My Favorite Movie 37
- Family Album 38
- What's In the Bag? 39
- Something I've Done 40
- When I Grow Up 41

• Formations 42
- Shape Formations 45
- Word Formations 46
- Number Formations 46
- Letter Formations 47
- Object Formations 47

• Line-Ups 48
- Line-Ups Characteristics 51
- Value Lines Cards 53
- Would You Live Forever? 56
- Cats Are Better Than Dogs 56
- Summer or Spring? 57
- Space Exploration or World Hunger? 57
- Cake or Ice Cream? 58
- President or Athlete 58
- Oceans or Rainforests 59
- Rich or Famous? 59

• Match Mine 60
- Farmyard Fun 63
- Cleo the Clown 64
- Class Picture 66
- Funny Faces 68
- Match My Tangram 72
- Match My Pythagoras Puzzle 73
- Our Community 74

• Pairs Compare 76
- Qualities of a Good Teammember 79
- A Good Cooperative Learning Team 80
- Wish Upon A Star 81
- I Wanna Visit 82
- My Favorite Music 83
- Season Activities 84
- Me and My Teammate 86
- Venn Diagram 87
- When I'm Alone 88
- My Favorite TV Shows 89

Table of  Contents

(continued)

• RoundRobin **90**
- My Birth Certificate 93
- My Family Portrait 94
- All About Me Book 95
- School Days Question Die 96
- Blackout 97
- Closest to Me 98
- Magic Stars 99
- Murder Mystery 100

• RoundTable **102**
- School and Baseball are 105
- Magic Kids 106
- A Good Look 107
- Build the Picture 108
- Our Team Likes 109
- Team Barnyard Scene 110
- Team Squiggle Art 111
- Team Shape Picture 112
- Shape Creation 113
- Build a Clown 114
- Making Words 115
- RoundTable Stories 116

• Same-Different **120**
- Recording Sheet 123
- Outer Space 124
- Pat the Raccoon 127
- Super Hero 130
- Pencil/Crayon 133

• Team Interview **134**
- Question Starters 137
- You're Rich and Famous 138
- Bedroom Door Hanger 139
- A Few of My Favorite Things 140
- The Perfect Vacation 141
- If You Could Play an Instrument 142
- Your Someone Special 142
- What Am I? 143

• Team Projects **144**
- Team Name 146
- Team Handshake and Cheer 146
- Team Logo or Banner 147
- Team Hats 147
- T-Shirt Poster 148
- Team Caps 149
- Team Shields 150
- Team Tower 151
- Pipe Cleaner Invention 151
- Team Box 152
- Silhouettes 152
- Teams Solve a Puzzle 153
- Write How to 153
- Spaghetti Space Station 154
- Team Mobile 154
- Mirror Walk 156
- Balloon Bounce 156
- Blindfolded 157
- The Worm 157

• Team Statements **158**
- A Hero is 161
- The Hardest Part of Growing Up is 162
- Our Team is Special because 163
- A Good Teammate is 164
- Listening is Important because ... 165
- School Would be Better if 166
- Working Together is Important because 167

• Three-Step Interview **168**
- Outlaw Interview 171
- On the Front Page 172
- Buy a Quality 173
- My Life 174
- My Partner's Life 175
- Qualities of a Friend 176
- Character Map 177

• Selected Resource List ..... _178_

Structures-at-a-Glance

4S Brainstorming

1. Teacher Assigns Roles
2. Teacher Announces Prompt
3. Students Generate Ideas

Blind Sequencing

1. Dealer Deals Cards
2. Students Describe Cards
3. Team Sequences Cards
4. Team Checks Sequence

Find-The-Fib

1. Students Write Three Statements
2. Students Read to Teammates
3. Teammates Discuss Statements
4. Teammates Guess & Celebrate

Kagans: *Cooperative Learning Structures for Teambuilding©*
Kagan Cooperative Learning • 1(800) WEE CO-OP

Structures-at-a-Glance

Formations

1. Teacher Announces Formation
2. Team Discussion
3. Teams Create Formation

Line-Ups

1. Teacher Describes the Line
2. Students Line Up
3. Team Discussion

Match Mine

1. Teams Build Buddy Barriers
2. Senders Create Design
3. Receivers Match Design
4. Team Checks Design

Kagans: *Cooperative Learning Structures for Teambuilding*©
Kagan Cooperative Learning • 1(800) WEE CO-OP

Pairs Compare

1. Teacher Presents Problem
2. RallyTable
3. Pairs Compare
4. Team Challenge

RoundRobin

1. Teacher Announces Topic
2. Students Take Turns Talking

RoundTable

1. Teacher Gives Directions
2. Students Take Turns

Kagans: *Cooperative Learning Structures for Teambuilding©*
Kagan Cooperative Learning • 1(800) WEE CO-OP

Structures-at-a-Glance

Same-Different

1. Teams Build Buddy Barriers
2. Distribute Materials
3. Students Discover Similarities & Differences
4. Pairs Compare Pictures

Team Interview

1. Teacher Announces a Topic
2. Students Interview First Teammate
3. Remaining Teammates Interviewed

Team Projects

1. Teacher Announces Project
2. Teams Complete Project

Kagans: *Cooperative Learning Structures for Teambuilding*©
Kagan Cooperative Learning • 1(800) WEE CO-OP

Team Statements

1. Think Time
2. Pairs Discuss
3. Individuals Write
4. RoundRobin
5. Team Statement
6. Teams Share

Three-Step Interview

1. A's Interview B's
2. B's Interview A's
3. RoundRobin

Preface

This book is written for you and your students. It is loaded with powerful cooperative learning structures and ready-to-use, proven teambuilding activities designed to transform student groups into caring and cooperative teams.

What is Teambuilding?

Teambuilding, as the name suggests, is the process of building teams. What we mean by building teams is not merely putting four students together to work. We mean turning a group of four students with different backgrounds and experiences into a cooperative and caring team.

There are five specific aims of teambuilding: 1) Getting Acquainted. When teammates are well acquainted, there is a friendly, positive team atmosphere, an atmosphere in which students feel comfortable being together and working together. 2) Team Identity. Creating a team identity gives students a sense of ownership, affiliation and solidarity. Teammates feel their team is special and unique. Students feel, "This is OUR team," "I am a member of the Brain Busters," and "We are all in this together; we are on the same team." 3) Mutual Support. Teammates need to feel mutually supported by one another. When students feel they share common goals, they are positively interdependent. Teammates are willing to help when help is requested and request help when needed. Teammates congratulate each others' success. 4) Valuing Differences. Teammates from diverse backgrounds with differing values, learning styles, skills not only need to learn to tolerate diversity, but actually learn to celebrate each member's uniqueness. Richer interaction, more creative products, and more cognitive flexibility result from teammates who value heterogeneity. 5) Developing Synergy. Working cooperatively unleashes a synergistic force enabling students to learn and do more than they ever could independently. Four heads are better than one. We are all smarter than any one of us. In teams, Together Everyone Achieves More!

When all five goals are achieved, teambuilding has been successful and a team emerges. There is no match for a well-functioning team. This book is loaded with activities to reach the five goals of teambuilding. Before we get to the activities, let's focus on the rationale for teambuilding, why we should do teambuilding in the class.

The Five Aims of Teambuilding

1) Getting Acquainted
2) Team Identity
3) Mutual Support
4) Valuing Differences
5) Developing Synergy

Why do Teambuilding?

Setting the Climate for Learning

There are three different ways we can structure our classrooms. We can make a competitive class, pitting our students against each other. We can create an individualistic classroom in which students work independently. Or we can build a cooperative classroom where students work together. A great deal of research has been done on how we should structure our classrooms. The research has established that the cooperative structure outperforms competitive and individualistic structures academically and socially, regardless of content or grade level.

Well, if students do better academically when they work cooperatively, shouldn't we use student teams at least part of the time? Yes. "Well, hold it," you say "I've been on a team, and we didn't work well together," or perhaps "I've tried teams in my class before and it just didn't work out." That's not a big surprise. Just putting people together doesn't ensure success. People can and often do have trouble working together. In our current educational system, many teachers (no fault to them) have defaulted to the traditional individualistic or competitive structures. Invariably, some students come to class with no experience or skills in working together. We do teambuilding to overcome the initial resistance, promote a positive team and classroom climate, and provide students the skills to work with others. Only when students are willing and able to work together will we maximize the learning potential of our students.

Only when students are willing and able to work together will we maximize the learning potential of our students.

Preparation for the Future

Teambuilding is important not just because it makes cooperative learning work, and not just because it results in higher academic achievement. Teambuilding is critical in preparing students with life skills for the 21st Century. Advancing technological complexity creates interdependence in the workplace. There is an exponential technological explosion

which is transforming the way we work and live. No one person alone builds a computer or even a component of a computer — the workplace of the future is teams coordinating their efforts with other teams. Are you a member or some type of team? It's likely. Three-fourths of US organizations have some employees who are members of identified working teams; over one-fourth of U.S. organizations have self-directed relatively autonomous teams which manage a wide range of functions, including setting work schedules, production quotas, and quality targets; purchasing equipment and services; conducting performance evaluations; budgeting, hiring, and firing.

Teambuilding skills are essential if our students of today will work well in the world of tomorrow which will be marked by dramatic diversity. Our world is

Teambuilding skills are essential if our students of today will work well in the world of tomorrow which will be marked by dramatic diversity.

rapidly becoming increasingly heterogeneous. Students who learn to work with others will function well in environments marked by diversity; those without teamwork skills will flounder. Ability to get along with others, especially those different from oneself, translates into the ability to land a job, keep a job, and excel.

Tearing Down Barriers

Perhaps the most compelling reason to do teambuilding is that it breaks down unnecessary barriers and allows individuals to deal with each other as people. School and society are becoming increasingly pluralistic. Although desegregation is court mandated, we are failing at integration. Young students come to school color-blind, willing to work and play together. Each school year, students become more and more polarized. It is an indictment of our traditional schooling practices that the more years of school students have had, the more they need teambuilding before they can work well together. As years go by, the "cool" kids look at the "nerds" with suspicion; the rich and poor see each other as "snobs" and "losers;" and students segregate into cliques and gangs based on race.

Sports is the exception. Why do students who would normally hold prejudices against each other become friends? In sports, teammates are truly interdependent. The success of one member of the team is positively correlated with the success of the team. Teammates value each others' unique set of skills and abilities as they pull together toward the common goal.

In the classroom we can harness interdependence. We don't have to always have students working alone with, "no talking." And we most definitely don't need to always pit students against each other! We can let

> **We are on the same team with the same goals; I understand your joys, your values, your pains; to me, you are no longer a "nerd" or a "loser" — you are me.**

students get to know one another as individuals and allow them to work on equal footing toward common goals. When we provide teambuilding, students tear down the needless barriers that keep them apart. Students get to know each other not by labels, the cost of their clothes, or the color of their skin, students come to know each other as people. We are on the same team with the same goals; I understand your joys, your values, your pains; to me, you are no longer a "nerd" or a "loser" — you are me.

When Do I Do Teambuilding?

Teambuilding activities are essential when teams are first formed, especially at the beginning of the school year, and each time new teams are formed. Teambuilding activities set a positive tone within the team and within the class. We recommend that heterogeneous teams be kept together for about six weeks; when new teams are formed, it is time to begin with some teambuilding activities. Often you will want to use random and homogeneous teams for brief activities or lessons. A quick teambuilder sets the right tone. The one or more minutes off academic curriculum translates to better academic curriculum acquisition because it creates the climate in which learning flourishes.

When energy dips, a teambuilder quickly energizes the class. When a team is not functioning well academically, a teambuilder often makes a remarkable difference. If a team is "bogged down," unable to make a decision, complete a project, or just plain tired of working, it is time for a teambuilder. At the beginning of the lesson which comes after lunch, when too much blood is in the stomach rather than the brain, a quick teambuilder can correct the balance. In the middle of that "block schedule," when concentration lags, a five minute teambuilder saves the rest of the lesson. We recommend using a teambuilder at a very minimum of twice a week; more often will probably improve class tone and academic achievement.

How to Get the Most Out of This Book

We selected fourteen favorite cooperative learning structures for teambuilding. Each structure promotes positive interaction with teammates. The book is arranged alphabetically by structure. For each structure, we have provided a description, illustrated step-by-step procedures, some hints, variations you may want to try and how the structure relates to the four basic principles of cooperative learning: Positive Interdependence, Individual Accountability, Equal Participation and Simultaneous Interaction (PIES). Following each structure are many fun, ready-to-use teambuilding activities with blackline masters to copy and hand out. To maximize the success of the activities, take the time familiarize yourself with the structure. When you are more familiar with the structure, you can better model and monitor students' interaction.

The cooperative learning structures described in this book are very strong teaching tools.

The cooperative learning structures described in this book are very strong teaching tools. Let's take one structure, Team Statements, as an example. In Team Statements, teammates work together through a series of specific steps to complete a statement. One of the provided activities is, "Our team is special because..." You can easily come up with many more teambuilding ideas by just plugging new teambuilding content into the same structure, "Together is better because..." or "A good teammate is..." or "We can win if..." This structure can also be meaningfully applied across the curriculum: In math, "To get the answer, you..." or in language arts, "The moral of the story is..." or in social studies, "Culture is..." To really get the most out of this book, don't just view this book as a collection of teambuilding activities (although it is quite a collection). Look at the underlying cooperative learning structures and imagine how you can use them to create new teambuilding activities and build learning for your students across the curriculum.

We hope you and your students have as much fun with these activities as we did creating and preparing them for you. If you and your students develop a new twist on any of these activities or have suggestions for new activities or structures, don't hesitate to drop us a line. We would love the input.

Happy Teambuilding!

Laurie Kagan

Laurie,
Miguel,
and Spencer Kagan

4S Brainstorming

The team becomes a think tank as each student—each with a special role—contributes to the team's "storm" of ideas.

In 4S Brainstorming, each student gets a role. The teacher announces the topic on which students are to brainstorm as many creative ideas as possible. For example, the teacher might say, "Your team is stranded on a deserted island and the only thing you have is a Swiss army knife. What will you use the knife for?" Teammates put their heads together and generate as many ideas as possible. The secretary records each idea on a different small piece of paper. Brainstorming can be used as an end itself for creative thinking or as a beginning for generating ideas for problem solving, discussing, writing.

For 4S Brainstorming, each student gets one of the following S roles (role cards on pages 5-6):

• **Speed Sergeant** ensures that teammates work fast, under time pressure, to come up with as many ideas as possible. The team member assigned this role says things like, "We only have one minute left." "Let's hurry!" "Let's get quicker with our responses."

• **Chief Support** makes sure all ideas are encouraged with no evaluation of ideas. Chief Support says things like: "All ideas are great!" "That's an excellent idea!" "I really like that!"

• **Sultan of Silly** encourages silly ideas. Having a good percent of silly ideas is very helpful in the flow of ideas, keeping the tone creative and in increasing the range of ideas. The silly idea may not be part of the final solution, but may well lead to an idea that is. The Sultan of Silly says things like, "Let's have a crazy idea!" "Can anyone think of something funny?" It is not the Sultan's job to provide all the silly ideas, rather he or she is to encourage teammates to come up with silly ideas.

• **Synergy Guru** encourages teammates to build on each others' ideas, saying things like, "Let's build on that." "Let's combine these ideas." The Synergy Guru is also the team Secretary, recording each idea on a separate slip of paper. In teams of five the Secretary is a fifth role; in teams of three the roles of Chief Support, Synergy Guru, and Secretary are combined.

4S Brainstorming is a strong teambuilder designed to release synergy and generate an uninhibited flow of ideas. Students build on each others' ideas, coming up with a storehouse of creative ideas or solutions to problems.

❶ Teacher Assigns Roles

Assign roles: *"Person 1, you will be the Speed Sergeant, Person 2..."* As you assign each role, have students generate and record associated gambits—things for that person to say and do. Students record gambits on the back of their role cards (e.g. on the back of Sergeant Support's role card it may say, "Great idea!" and "Wow!").

3 Students Generate Ideas

In teams, students generate ideas. Remind students of their roles and gambits. The Secretary is not to stack or hold the slips of paper, but rather to lay them out as the team "covers the table" with ideas.

2 Teacher Announces Prompt

Announce a topic which prompts students to generate creative ideas. A prompt should have no right or wrong answers; rather it should be open-ended enough for students to come up with loads of creative ideas. *"Your team needs to raise $200 in the next week to go on a field trip. What are all the things you could do to raise the money?"*

H i n t s

★ **Model the Roles.** Have a team model the four roles and have students come up with gambits to fulfill each role.
★ **Role Cards.** Have each role on a role card, with the role name on the front and the gambits on the back. Folded slips of paper make nice role tents. Store the role cards in a team tub and pull them out when it's time to brainstorm.
★ **Open-ended Prompt.** Make sure the prompt allows students to generate many ideas.

Rotating Secretary

Rather than have only one member on the team be the secretary, use a Rotating Recorder (have the teammates each in turn record the next new idea).

Think-Pad Brainstorming

To increase simultaneity and the number of responses, use Think-Pad Brainstorming. Each teammember gets a think-pad or at least eight slips of paper. Students write down each new idea they come up with on a new slip, call out the idea, and place the slip in the center of the table.

Class Brainstorming

Class Brainstorming involves the whole class in the brainstorming session. The teacher (or a student) is the recorder. Students call out ideas as they come up with them. For more structure, have all students with an idea to share stand up. They sit when they share their idea or if someone else shares their same idea. Alternatively have the first three minutes for only Student Ones, the next three minutes for Student Twos and so on.

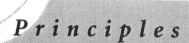

Principles

Teammates build on each others' ideas. Ideas trigger more ideas.

Students are accountable to teammates for generating and recording ideas. Students may also be held accountable for their ideas by having each students' contributions recorded on a separate sheet or in a different color.

Students should participate about equally. The roles help equalize participation. If equal participation is an important issue, have students generate ideas using RoundRobin.

Each team generates ideas simultaneously. Simultaneity is increased even more in Think-Pad Brainstorming, as all students may be active at once.

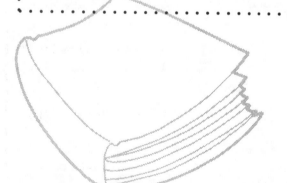

4S Brainstorming

Brainstorming Role Cards

Cut out cards and fold them in half. Use role cards for brainstorming.

Speed Sergeant's Job:
Get the team to come up with ideas quickly.

Say things like:
- "We only have one minute left."
- "Let's hurry!"
- "Let's get faster responses."
- ...

Fold

Speed Sergeant

Chief Support's Job:
Make sure all ideas are supported with no evaluation.

Say things like:
- "All ideas are great!"
- "That's an excellent idea!"
- "I really like that!"
- ...

Fold

Chief Support

Brainstorming Role Cards

Cut out cards and fold them in half. Use role cards for brainstorming.

Sultan of Silly's job:
Encourage teammates to come up with silly ideas.

Say things like:
- "Let's have a crazy idea!"
- "Can anyone think of something funny?"
- "We need a silly idea."
- •
- •

--- Fold ---

Sultan of Silly

Synergy Guru's job:
Encourage teammates to build on each other's ideas. Record the team's ideas.

Say things like:
- "Let's build on that."
- "Let's combine these ideas."
- "Can we staircase off that?"
- •
- •

--- Fold ---

Synergy Guru

Team Mascot

Cut out all the Team Mascot Pieces on the other page. In your team, build your team mascot. Then brainstorm ideas below. Use the back for more ideas.

1. What is your mascot's name?

_____

_____

_____

_____

_____

2. What do you do together?

_____

_____

_____

_____

3. What does your mascot eat?

_____

_____

_____

_____

_____

_____

_____

4. What bizarre things does your mascot do?

_____

_____

_____

_____

_____

Team Mascot Pieces

Cut out these pieces and create a team mascot.

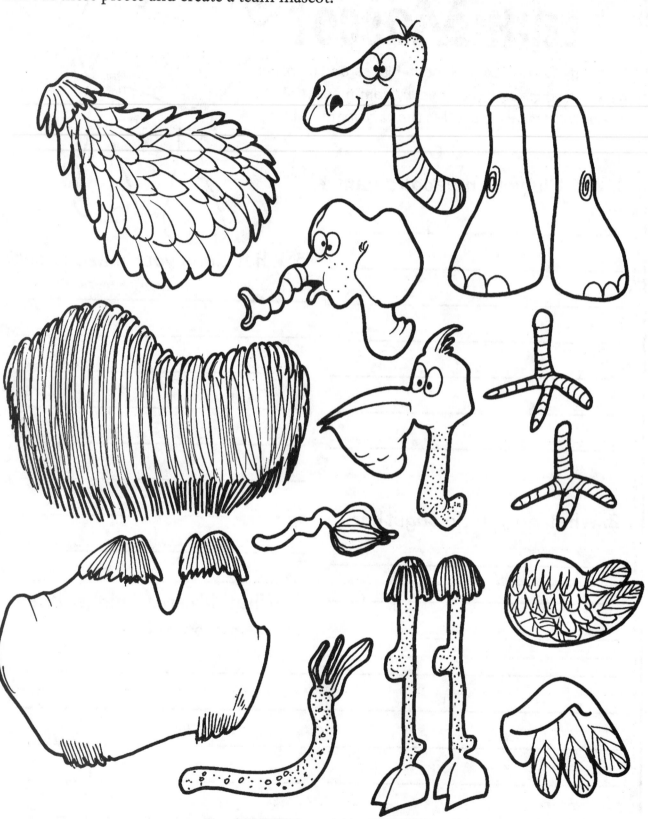

On a Deserted Island with Only a Belt

Your team is shipwrecked and wakes up on a deserted island. You are the only ones on the island. The only tool you have is one belt. Brainstorm how your team will use the belt to make life easier.

One Million Bucks

Your team wins one million bucks in the lottery. Brainstorm what you will do with all that money.

Team Name Train

Cut out the train role cards below. Everyone on the team gets one role card. Don't show anyone your secret role. Do what your train role card says as you brainstorm ideas for a team name. See how many team names your team can come up with. Use the back for more team names.

_____   _____

_____   _____

_____   _____

_____   _____

_____   _____

_____   _____

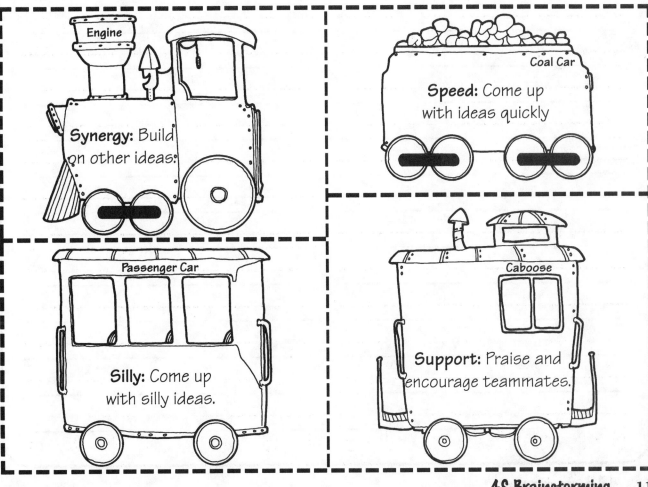

Engine

Synergy: Build on other ideas.

Coal Car

Speed: Come up with ideas quickly

Passenger Car

Silly: Come up with silly ideas.

Caboose

Support: Praise and encourage teammates.

The Perfect Weekend

The weekend is coming up! Brainstorm ideas to make it the perfect weekend.

Famous Scientist

Your team of scientists wants to contribute to the improvement of the quality of life on earth. What will your team invent, create or do to make the earth a better place to live?

School of the Future

Millions of students go to school each year. Your team is elected to design the school of the future. What will your team do to improve the school of the future?

4S Brainstorming   13

Blind Sequencing

Teams work to sequence cards in their proper order, but there is a catch—each student gets his or her own cards, and no one else can see what's on them!

The teacher prepares sequencing cards. Content on the cards may be fun teambuilding (frames of a cartoon strip) or academic (historical events or steps of solving a problem). Each team receives their cards face down so no one can see what's on the cards. One student on each team, the dealer, distributes the cards to teammates, face down. Each student marks the back of his or her card with a special mark (or initials) so each knows which cards belong to whom. Students look at their cards, without showing them to anyone. Teammates take turns describing their own cards. The team attempts to sequence the cards, placing them upside down on the table, one at a time, in order. No card is placed unless all teammates agree. Teammates continue to sequence the cards until the team agrees that the cards are in the correct sequence. Teams turn over the cards and check to see if they have correctly sequenced their cards.

Blind Sequencing creates strong interdependence among teammates. Each teammate must do a good job of describing their card if the team is to succeed.

1 Dealer Deals Cards

One student is assigned the role of dealer. The dealer's job is to equally distribute the cards among teammembers. The dealer deals the cards face down making sure no one can see the cards. When students get their cards, they are to mark the back of the cards to identify them as their cards. Students can use initials, a number, a letter or a geometric shape.

2 Students Describe Cards

In turn, each student describes his or her cards to the team. Students describe the cards as well as possible in an attempt to make it easy for the team to sequence the cards.

4 Team Checks Sequence

When the team thinks they have properly sequenced the cards, they flip over the cards and check to see how they did. If the sequence is correct, they celebrate with a team cheer. If the sequence is incorrect, they correct it and discuss what went wrong and how they could do better next time.

3 Team Sequences Cards

After all the cards have been described, the team works together to put the cards in the proper order. Students lay out the cards on the table one at a time, face down in the order they think they belong. No card is set on the table unless all teammates agree. If the team gets stuck, only the original card holder can peek at the card and describe it to the team.

Hints

★ **Face Down.** If students see each others' cards, it may ruin the activity. Tell students not to peek at the cards when they are initially face down and have students conceal their cards from teammates.

★ **Peeking Rule.** If teams are having difficulty sequencing the cards, students may peek at a card they have already laid down and describe it to the team.

★ **Distributing Cards.** To save time distributing cards, rather than placing the cards on each team table, have Student Threes come get a set of cards for their team.

★ **Students Prepare Cards.** Rather than the teacher preparing the cards, have each team prepare a set of Blind Sequencing cards. Teams trade with other teams and can play several times.

★ **Start Easy.** When first trying this structure, start easy. Give each student only one card. Introduce more cards as students get better at sequencing the cards.

Sequencing

Sequencing is the same as Blind Sequencing except students can see each others cards. In Sequencing, to ensure equal participation, it is important that no one may touch a card except for the original card holder.

Team Sequencing Line-Ups

Each student on the team gets one card with something to sequence. Teammates physically line up based on the sequence of their cards.

Class Sequencing Line-Ups

Each student in the class gets one card with something to sequence. The whole class lines up based on the sequence of their cards.

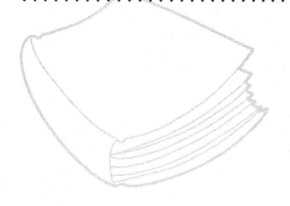

Principles

Students are strongly interdependent because students can't see each other's cards.

Students are accountable to the team for describing the cards well and for placing his or her cards in sequence.

If possible, every student receives the same number of cards to describe and place.

Teams work simultaneously, sequencing the cards.

Blind Sequencing

Kagans: *Cooperative Learning Structures for Teambuilding*©
Kagan Cooperative Learning • 1(800) WEE CO-OP

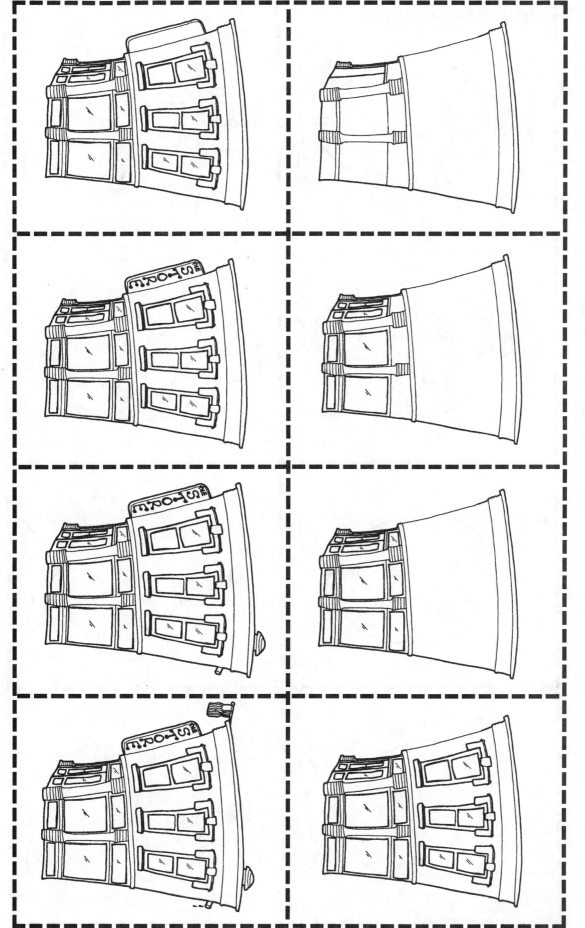

Cut out cards. Sequence the cards from least detailed to most detailed.

Sequence the Good News Bear

Cut out cards. Sequence the cards from least detailed to most detailed.

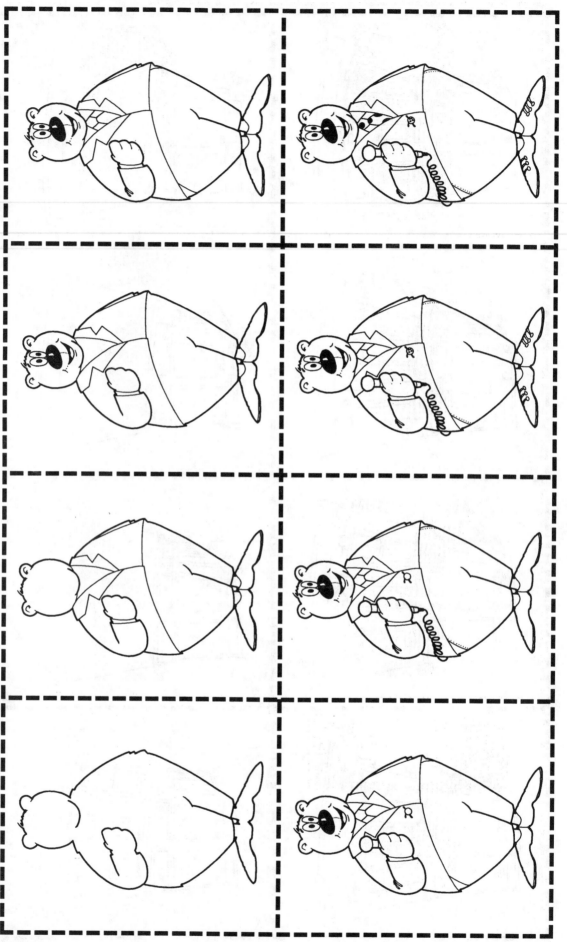

Cut out the cards. Sequence cards so each shape fits into the prior shape.

Blind Sequencing 19

Sequence the Fractions

Cut out cards. Sequence fractions from least to greatest.

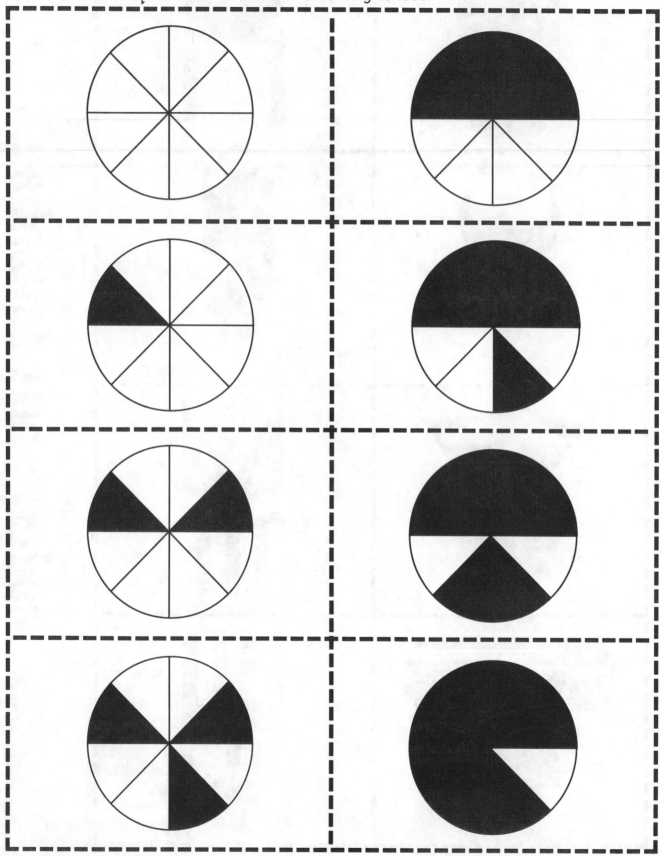

Sequence the Decimals

Cut out cards. Sequence decimals from least to greatest.

.012	.624
.126	.628
.377	.999
.501	1.001

Sequence the Train

Cut out cards. Sequence the train. Pay special attention to the hitches.

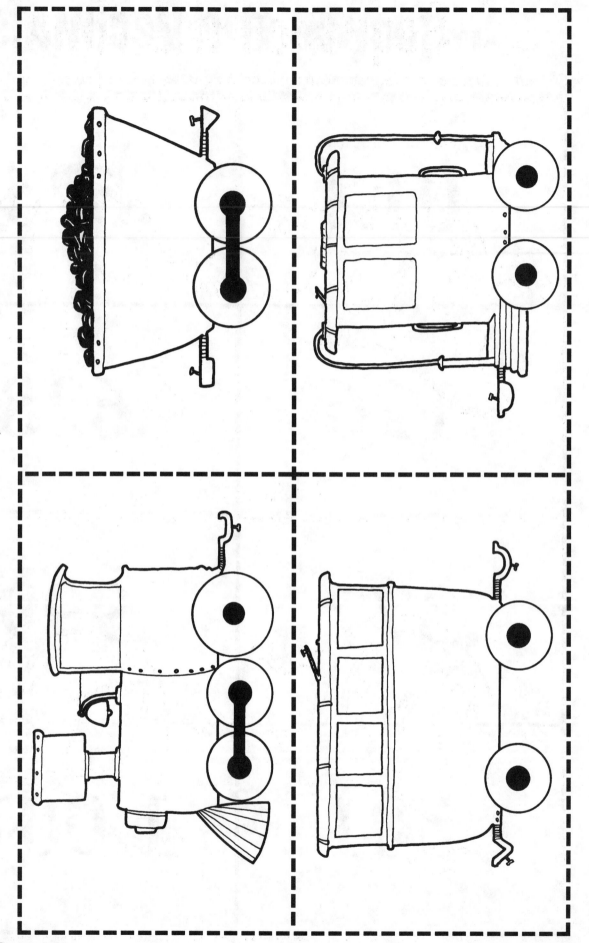

Sequence the Time

Cut out cards. Sequence the clocks from the morning to the evening.

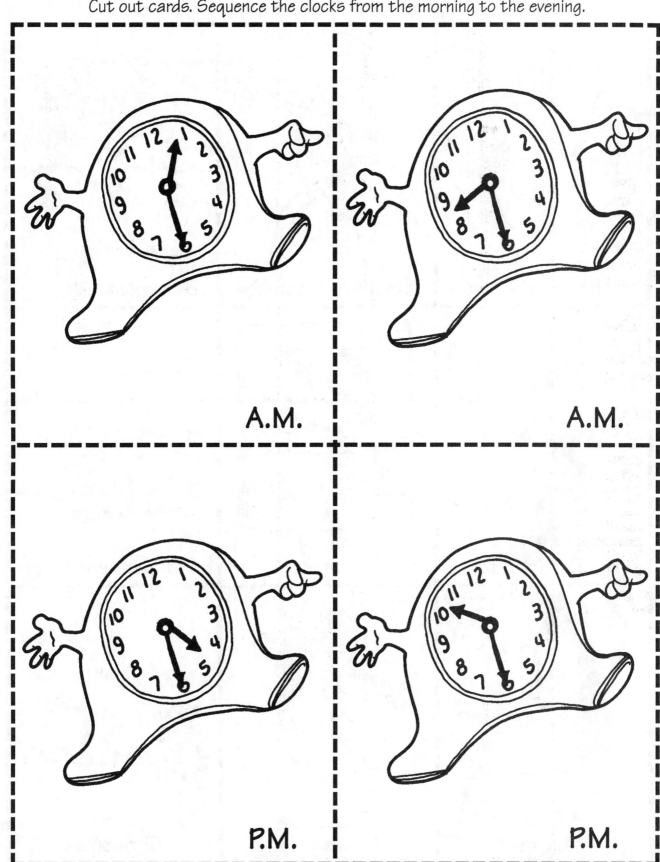

A.M.

A.M.

P.M.

P.M.

Sequence the Holidays

Cut out cards. Sequence the holidays by calendar occurrence.

New Year's Day

Lincoln's Birthday

St. Valentine's Day

St. Patrick's Day

Easter

Independence Day

Halloween

Thanksgiving

Christmas

24 **Blind Sequencing**

Sequence the Ant Farm

Cut out cards. One student reads, "How to Make an Ant Farm" to the team, then the team works together to sequence the steps for making an ant farm.

How to Make an Ant Farm. First, you will need a hammer, nails, wood and glass. Build the frame with the wood and slide the glass in on both sides. Then, glue the glass to the frame on both ends. Add some sand, then add some water to moisten the sand. Add some grass on the top. Put the ants in, cover up the farm with screen and a rubber band.

Find-the-Fib

The team shares some laughs as one teammate presents statements to their team and the other teammates work together to figure out which one of the statements is the fib.

Each student writes down three statements. Two of the statements are true and one is a fib. For a getting acquainted activity, students write the three statements about themselves. Alternatively, academic content may be used. One student reads his or her three statements to the team. The other teammates huddle to discuss the statements, trying to determine which one of the statements is not true. If the team guesses the fib, the student reading his or her statement applauds teammates. If the team does not guess the fib, the team applauds the fibber.

Find-the-Fib is great for getting acquainted as teammates learn personal information about each other. Find-the-Fib promotes a positive tone among teammates as they have fun trying to "find the fib."

1 Students Write Three Statements

Have each student write three statements. *"We are going to play Find-the-Fib, so everyone needs to come up with three statements about themselves. Two of the statements are unbelievable facts and one statement is a believable fib."*

2 Students Read to Teammates

When students are done writing their statements, call a number and have that student stand and read his or her three statements to the team.

4 Teammates Guess & Celebrate

The team presents its guess. If the team correctly guesses the fib, the fibber applauds teammates. If the team guesses incorrectly, they applaud the fibber.

Play again: The teammate on the left of the fibber stands and the team repeats steps two through four until time runs out or until each student has had a chance to present his or her statements.

3 Teammates Discuss Statements

The team puts their heads together to reach consensus on which one of the three statements is the fib. *"Put your heads together and decide together which one is the fib. You have not made a decision until you come up with a guess you can all live with."*

Hint

★ **Make Corrections.** Make sure students correct the fib so students remember correct information.

Fact-or-Fiction

In Fact-or-Fiction, each student comes up with one statement instead of three. The statement is either a believable lie or an unlikely truth. Teammates attempt to guess if the statement is fact or fiction. Fact-or-Fiction is well suited for young students who have difficulty remembering three facts at once.

Find-the-Fibs

To make the game more challenging for older students, students come up with three statements. Either none, one, two or three of the statements are fibs. Teams try to figure out which statements are fibs.

Team Find-the-Fib & Team Fact-or-Fiction

In the team variation, teammates work together to come up with three statements for Find-the-Fib or one for Fact-or-Fiction. One student on the team is chosen as a team representative to present the statement(s) to the class. Other teams try to figure out which statement is a fib (Find-the-Fib) or whether it is true or false (Fact-or-Fiction).

Class Find-the-Fib & Class Fact-or-Fiction

Instead of playing in teams, have one student present their three statements for Find-the-Fib or one statement for Fact-or-Fiction to the whole class. Each team must reach consensus on which statement they think is a fib (Find-the-Fib) or whether the statement is true or false (Fact-or-Fiction).

Response Modes

• **Thumbs Up, Thumbs Down.** Students can vote with their thumbs — thumbs up for a true statement or fact; thumbs down for a fib or fiction.

• **Finger Responses.** Students signal their guess by holding up one, two or three fingers.

• **Card Responses.** Students hold up cards with the number corresponding to the fib.

Principles

Students are interdependent in guessing the fib. Clever thinking by any teammate helps all the teammates.

Each student is accountable to teammates for coming up with and presenting his or her statements.

Students participate about equally. Each student presents his or her statements.

Each team simultaneously plays Find-the-Fib.

Find-the-Fib

Kagans: *Cooperative Learning Structures for Teambuilding*©
Kagan Cooperative Learning • 1(800) WEE CO-OP

Find-the-Fib Response Cards

Cut out cards and use them as response cards for Find-the-Fib.

#1 is the fib

#2 is the fib

#3 is the fib

Fact-or-Fiction Response Cards

Cut out cards and use them as response cards for Fact or Fiction.

It's fact!

It's fiction!

My Life on Screen

Fill out the film strip. Don't forget to include one fib. Cut out the film strip and the T.V. screen. Make two slits in the T.V. screen and pull the film strip through the T.V. as you share your life with teammates. See if your teammates can pick out the fib.

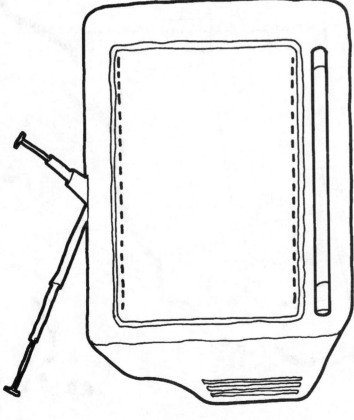

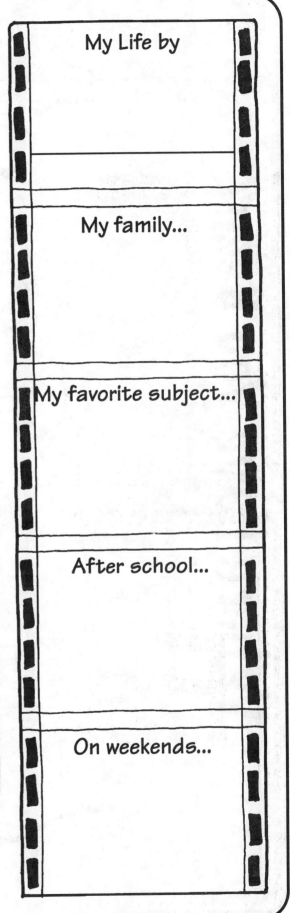

My Life by

My family...

My favorite subject...

After school...

On weekends...

Where Have You Been?

Mark where you have been on the map of the United States. Be sure to include important locations (like Disneyland) and one fib. See if your teammates can pick out the fib.

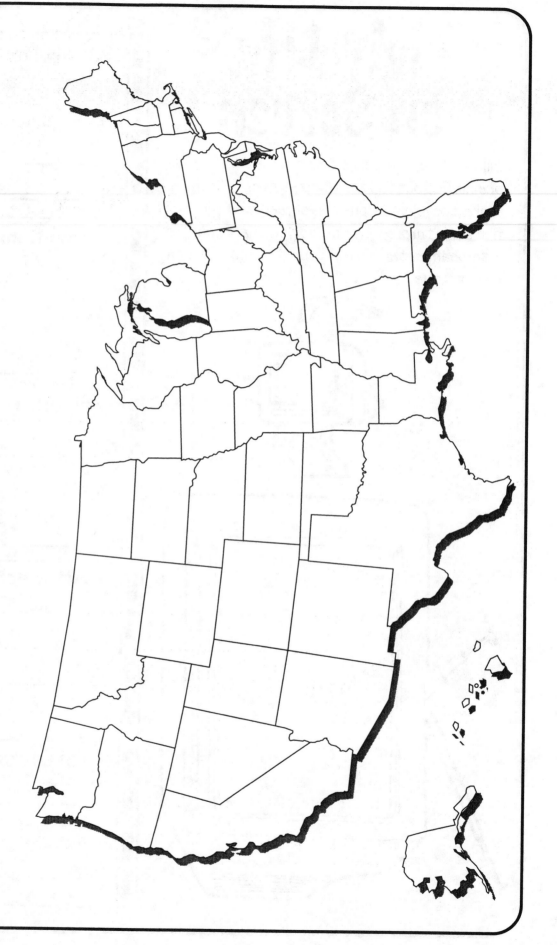

32   **Find-the-Fib**

I'm Outta Here!

If you could live somewhere else or with someone else, where would it be and why? Don't forget to include a fib. See if your teammates can pick out the fib.

_____
_____
_____

_____
_____
_____

_____
_____
_____

Find-the-Fib   33

The Big Book of Names

Hello, My Name Is...

If you could change your name, what would you change your name to? Why? Don't forget to include a fib. See if your teammates can pick out the fib.

1 Name_____

Why? _____

_____

2 Name_____

Why? _____

_____

3 Name_____

Why? _____

_____

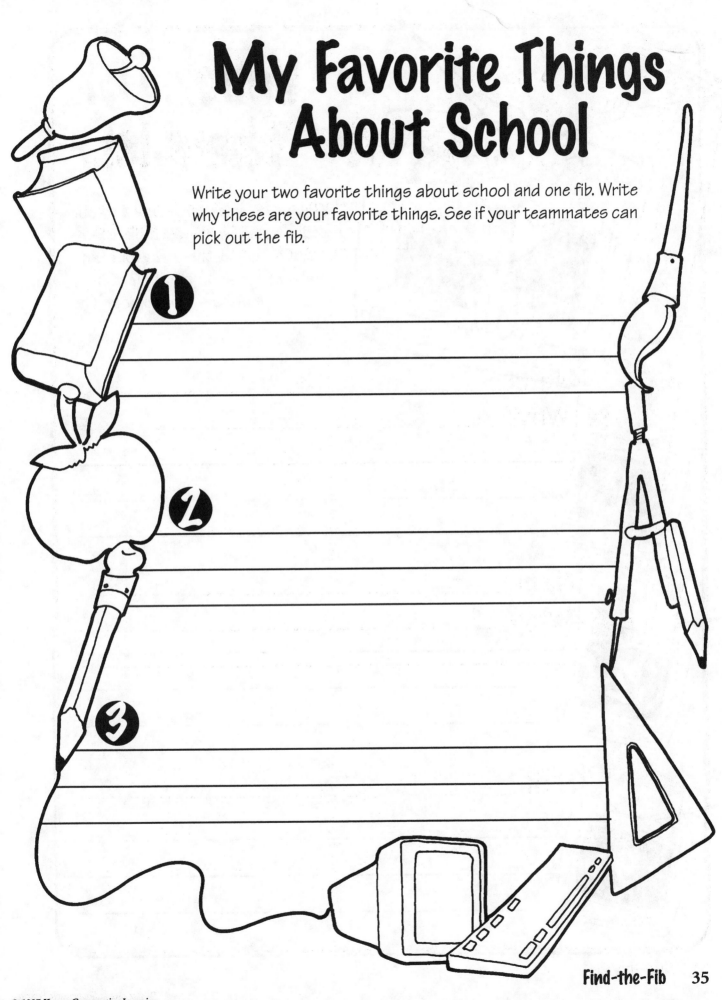

My Favorite Things About School

Write your two favorite things about school and one fib. Write why these are your favorite things. See if your teammates can pick out the fib.

1

2

3

You're On The Air!

Write a commercial about why your team would want you as a team-member. Write three reasons and make one reason not true. See if your teammates can pick out the fib.

1

2

3

My Favorite Movie

Write the titles of your favorite movies and why they are your favorites. Make one of the three movies a fib. See if you can fool your teammates with the fib.

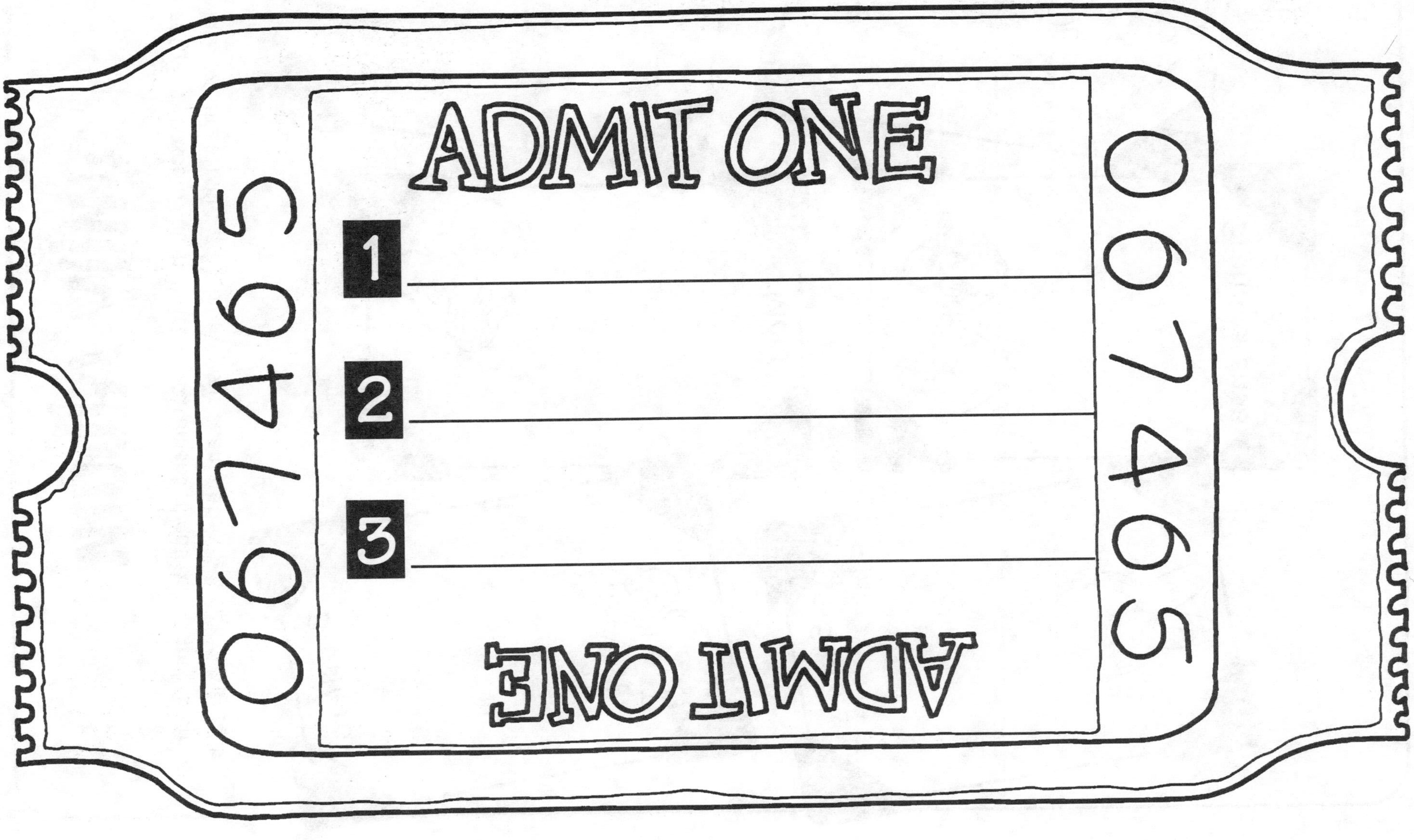

067465

ADMIT ONE

1

2

3

ADMIT ONE

067465

Family Album

Choose at least three boxes to fill in. Write a statement about each family member you select. Make one statement a fib. See if your teammates can pick out the fib.

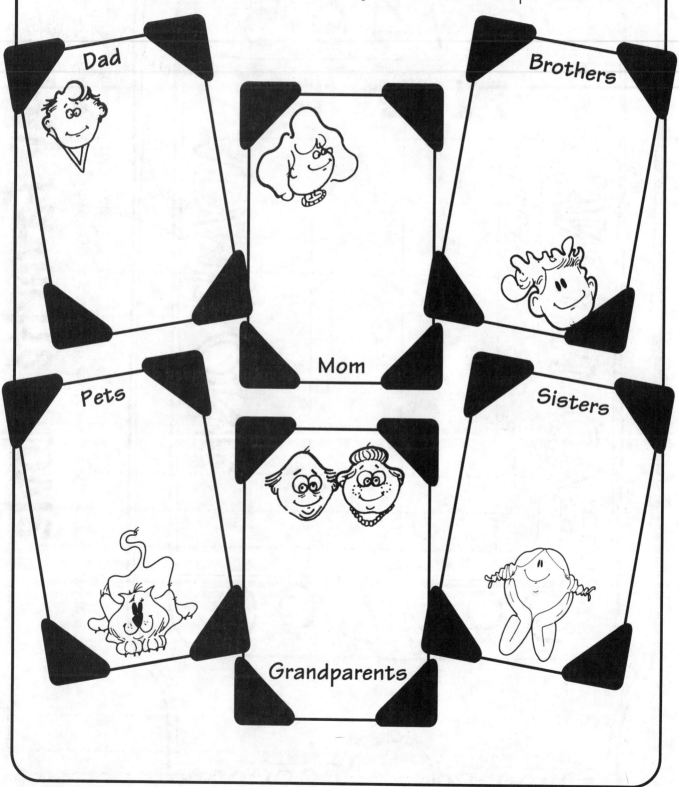

What's In the Bag?

Everyone on the team brings three small items from home and puts them in a brown paper bag. On the front of the bag, write what two of the objects are and write a fib for the third object. Without peeking in the bag, each teammate feels what's in your bag. Teammates discuss what the third item really is and guess which item is the fib. Use the space below to record the items in each bag and the fib.

Bag 1
1.
2.
3.
Fib:

Bag 2
1.
2.
3.
Fib:

Bag 3
1.
2.
3.
Fib:

Bag 4
1.
2.
3.
Fib:

Find-the-Fib   39

Something I've Done

Describe something you've done in the past and illustrate it in the banner below. It can be real or fake. Your teammates guess whether you are telling the truth or not.

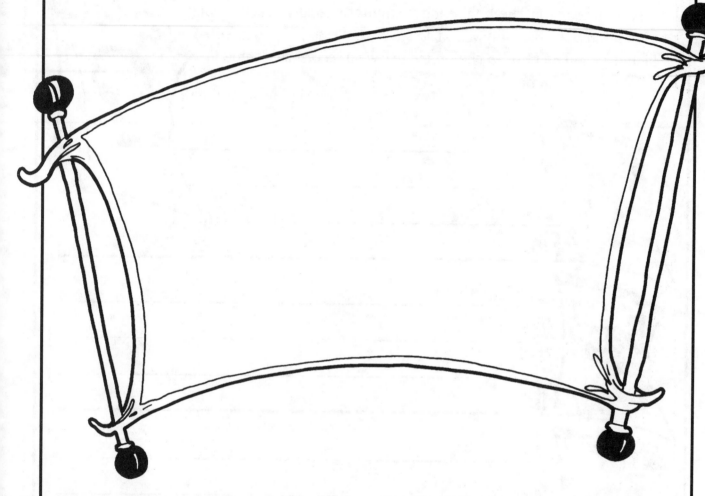

Something I've done is...

_____

_____

_____

_____

_____

_____

_____

When I Grow Up...

Fill in what you want to be when you grow up. It can be fake or real. Draw a quick sketch of the career in the box. Write why you chose that career. Your teammates guess whether you are telling the truth or not.

Because...

_____

_____

_____

_____

_____

Formations

Teammates excitedly coordinate efforts, positioning themselves to create a challenging team formation.

In Formations, the teacher presents a challenging formation. "Using just your bodies, spell the word TEAM." Students take some time to plan their formation, deciding where each student should be and what each student should do. Once students have a plan, they then work together to make the formation. More advanced formations include, sound and movement. For example, the letters of TEAM may first be separate, come together to spell the word, and then walk off together.

Formations is a strong teambuilder because it is a fun team energizer and develops mutual support among teammates. Students must coordinate their efforts to accomplish the team goal of making the formation come alive.

1 Teacher Announces Formation

The teacher announces the formation and sets the ground rules. *"A trapezium is like a team. There are four sides, like four teammates. Just as every teammember is unique, a trapezoid has no parallel sides; yet together, the unparallel sides come together to form a uniform quadrilateral. Form a team trapezium with only your bodies. Everyone must be included."*

2 Team Discussion

Teams take some time to plan how they are going to create the formation. They decide who will do what and how to include everyone.

③ Teams Create Formation

The team works together to create the team formation.

Hints

★ **Start Easy.** Have teams do a few simple formations before working up to more complex ones.
★ **Use Visuals.** Show teams a picture of what they are to form.
★ **Use Props.** Allow teams to use available props in the classroom. Turn the team formation into a performance piece of art.
★ **Everyone Participates.** Everyone on the team must be involved in the formation.
★ **Safety Tip.** If students are going to use props, make sure that they are not going to do anything potentially dangerous like stacking chairs or desks.
★ **Open Space.** Some formations may require some open space. Some formations are better created outside.

Class Formations
Instead of having each team do a formation, give the entire class one formation.

Silent Formations
Have the class or the team do the formation without talking.

Guess-the-Formation
Give each team a different formation. Each team creates their formation and other teams try to guess the formation.

Team Charades
Have teams act out different events. This can be done like charades. The team can act something out for another team or for the class to guess.

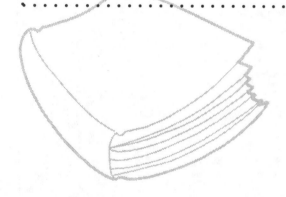

Principles

Teammates need each other; no one teammate can create the formation alone.

Each student is accountable to the team for contributing to the team formation.

Student are equal participants in the team formation.

Each team simultaneously plans their formation.

Formations

Kagans: *Cooperative Learning Structures for Teambuilding*®
Kagan Cooperative Learning • 1(800) WEE CO-OP

Shape Formations

Have teams form various shapes.

Form a square.

Form a circle.

Form a right angle triangle.

Word Formations

Have teams form four letter words.

(Boat)

Number Formations

Have teams form four digit numbers.

(1972)

Letter Formations

Have teams form
one letter.

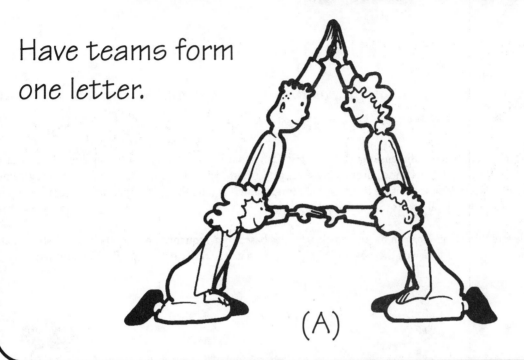

(A)

Object Formations

Have teams form
common objects or
symbols.

(Ice Cream Cone)

Line-Ups

Students find they each occupy a unique position in the team and teammates can see at a glance where everyone stands.

In Line-Ups, the teacher announces a dimension upon which students may line up. The students may line up on a characteristic like "height" in which case teams line up from tallest to shortest (Line-Ups). The students may line up on agreement or disagreement (Value Lines) with a value issue like, "Capital Punishment is a good thing." Or the students may line up in a sequence as in a sequence of historical events (Sequencing Line-Ups).

Line-Ups is a flexible structure. Line-Ups can be fun, quick activities based on a sequence of student characteristics, or they may be a springboard for students to clarify their own values and appreciate the differing values of their teammates.

2 Students Line Up

Students position themselves in the line-up by finding where they stand relative to teammates.

1 Teacher Describes the Line

Announce a dimension upon which teammates vary. *"Line up from youngest to oldest."*

3 Team Discussion

Students sit down in their teams to discuss the topic. "What do you like about your birthday? Would you prefer to be younger or older?"

Hints

★ **RoundRobin Paraphrase.** To promote respectful listening, have each student state their feelings or thoughts about the line-up topic. Next, the student to the left of the last student to share paraphrases what that student has shared before sharing their own ideas. Each student is paraphrased by one other student.

★ **Value Statements.** For Value Lines, make a statement on a controversial issue, and indicate the end points of the line as "Agree" and "Disagree."

★ **Spectrum Topics.** Use topics that create a continuum of stances. Don't use topics that separate students into distinct groups like eye color or sex.

Class Line-Ups

Rather than having students line up in teams, have students find their place in the class line up. Use Class Line-Ups also with values, characteristics and sequencing.

Value Lines

Students line up relative to their teammates based on where they stand on an issue. The poles are usually agree/disagree or like/dislike.

Sequencing Line-Ups

Have students line up to sequence events. Students are given cards with numbers, letters, words, events, steps or stages.

Folded Line-Ups

Lines can be folded to have students with different characteristics or values meet and discuss. To fold the line up, have the students at one end of the line walk over to the other end. Students follow the leader so that when they stop, each is across from a new partner. New partners shake hands and discuss the issue.

Share & Fold

Before folding a Line-Up, have students first discuss the issue with a partner next to them in the line-up. This provides students support for their stance as well as providing them with better ideas to share with their new partner after the line is folded.

Split & Slide Line-Ups

The line-up is split in the middle. Half of the line takes three steps forward. The line then slides down so that every student faces another student. Students who were in the middle of the line-up are now faced with students from the ends. After the split and slide, students discuss with their partner why they took the stance they did, or topics provided by the teacher.

Paraphrase Passport

In Folded Value Line-Ups, students discuss issues with students of different viewpoints. To validate what the other student is saying, play Paraphrase Passport. Students must paraphrase what their partner said before speaking. Paraphrasing promotes active listening skills—it holds students individually accountable for listening.

Praise Passport

Praise Passport is the same as Paraphrase Passport except students must praise something their partner said before speaking. Students feel that their perspective is worthy when it is appreciated. Praise Passport makes students look for virtues in a perspective different from their own. Remind students that they do not have to agree with a point of view to appreciate how well it is stated, the thought which went into it, or the strength of the feelings behind it. Advanced students are told "no generic praisers." "Good idea" can be said of any idea; it is not as strong a praiser as "Your idea was clever because…"

Principles

Students' ideas are enriched when they share with students who are like them and different from them.

Students are accountable to their partners for sharing. Paraphrase Passport holds students accountable for listening.

Students all participate in the line-up. During the team discussion, use RoundRobin so they hear from everyone.

Teams are simultaneously lining up and discussing.

Line-Ups

Kagans: *Cooperative Learning Structures for Teambuilding*©
Kagan Cooperative Learning • 1 (800) WEE CO-OP

Line-Ups Characteristics

Have students line up on the attributes described on the cards.

Alphabetical Order

Line up in alphabetical order by:
- First name
- Last name
- Middle name
- Favorite sport
- Favorite color
- Favorite food

Date

Line up by the date of:
- Your birthday
- Date of favorite holiday
- Favorite day of the week
- Favorite month
- Favorite year
- Favorite age

Time

Line up in order of the time you:

- Woke up this morning
- Went to bed last night
- Had dinner last night
- Time it takes you to walk to school
- Time it takes you to get ready for school

Size

Line up in order of:

- Tallest to shortest
- Shortest to tallest
- Shoe size
- Head circumference
- Length of hair
- Hand size
- Arm span
- Ear size

Line-Ups Characteristics

Have students line up on the attributes described on the cards.

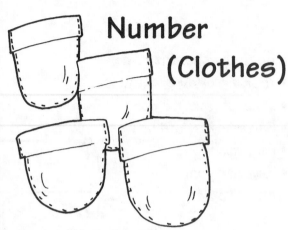

Number
(Clothes)

Line up in order of:
• Number of pockets
• Number of buttons
• Number of stripes
• Number of shoe lace holes

Number
(Siblings)

Line up by:
• Number of brothers
• Number or sisters
• Number of aunts
• Number of uncles
• Number of cousins

Pets

Line up in order of :
• Number of pets
• Alphabetical by pet's name
• Size of pet
• Years had pet

Weight

Line up in order of:
• Weight of left shoe
• Weight of backpack
• Weight of lunch

Value Lines Cards

Each teammate gets all 3 cards. Select your card and find your position in the Value Line.

Value Lines Cards

Each teammate gets all 3 cards. Select your card and find your position in the Value Line.

Agree

Not Sure

Disagree

Value Lines Cards

Each teammate gets all 3 cards. Select your card and find your position in the Value Line.

For

Not Sure

Against

Would You Live Forever?

Think whether or not you would live forever. Mark an X on your sheet where you stand. Take turns sharing your answer with teammates.

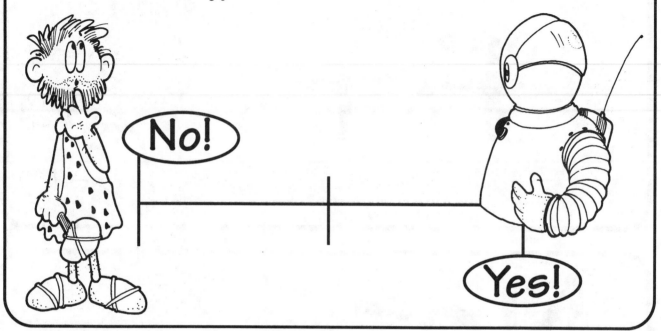

Cats Are Better Than Dogs

Think whether or not you agree or disagree with this statement. Mark an X on your sheet where you stand. Take turns sharing your answer with teammates.

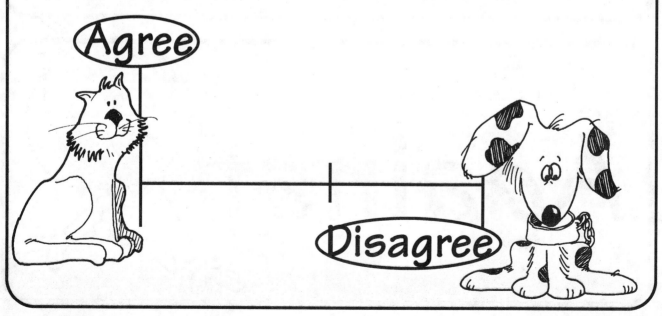

Summer or Spring?

Think whether you prefer summer or spring. Mark an X on your sheet where you stand. Take turns sharing your answer with teammates.

Summer   Spring

Space Exploration or World Hunger?

Do do you think space exploration is more important than ending world hunger? Mark an X on your sheet where you stand. Take turns sharing your answer with teammates.

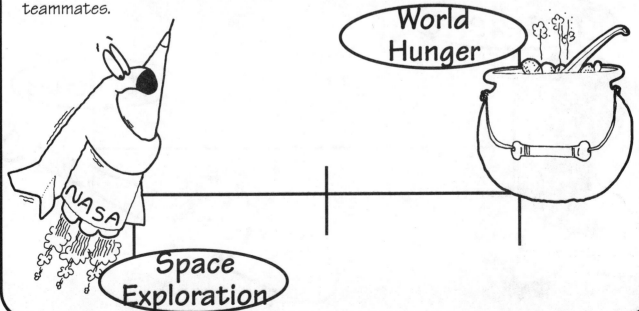

World Hunger

Space Exploration

Cake or Ice Cream?

Do you prefer cake or ice cream? Mark an X on your sheet where you stand. Take turns sharing your answer with teammates.

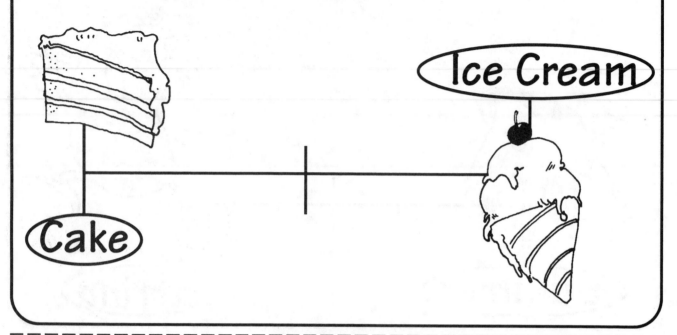

President or Athlete?

Would you rather be the President or a famous athlete? Mark an X on your sheet where you stand. Take turns sharing your answer with teammates.

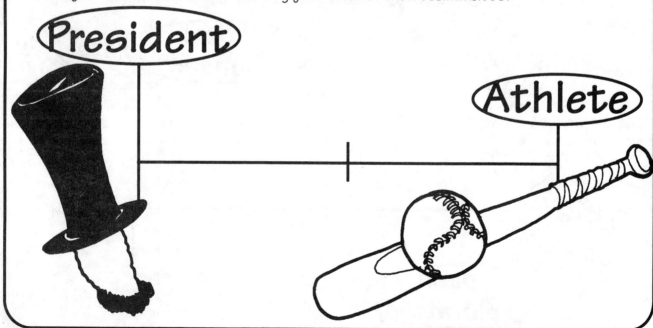

Oceans or Rainforests?

Do you think it is more important to protect our oceans or rainforests? Mark an X on your sheet where you stand. Take turns sharing your answer with teammates.

Rainforests

Oceans

Rich or Famous?

Would you rather be rich or famous? Mark an X on your sheet where you stand. Take turns sharing your answer with teammates.

Rich

Famous

Match Mine

The two "Senders" arrange gamepieces on a gameboard. The challenge is for the two "Receivers" to match the Senders' arrangement without seeing it.

The team sets up a file folder barrier with a pair of students on each side of the barrier. Each pair gets an identical set of materials. For instance, the materials can be a sheet of graph paper for a gameboard, and cut-out colored geometric shaped gamepieces. One pair (the Senders) arranges the geometric shapes on their sheet of graph paper. When the senders have arranged the geometric shapes, then the other two (the Receivers) try to match the arrangement of the Senders. The Senders describe their arrangement as the Receivers try to match it exactly. When the whole team thinks that they have correctly made a match, the Senders and Receivers compare their work to see how well they did. If the gamepieces are arranged identically, the team celebrates their success. If the gamepieces don't match, teammates congratulate their efforts, then discuss how they could have communicated better to make the match.

Match Mine is a great teambuilding structure because the team is strongly interdependent. Students must pull together to reach the common team objective—making a match.

1 Teams Build Buddy Barriers

Each team builds a barrier. File folder barriers are very simple to build. Give each team two file folders and one paper clip. They clip the file folders together at the top with a paper clip, spread the base and Presto! they have a stand-alone buddy barrier.

2 The Senders Create Design

The Senders work together to arrange their gamepieces (tangrams, pattern blocks, card stock cut-outs, color tiles, or rubber bands on a geoboard).

4 Team Checks Design

When the whole team thinks that the Receivers have accurately matched the Senders' design, they compare their work. If the designs are identical, the team celebrates their success. If they don't match, they congratulate their efforts, then discuss how they could have communicated better to make the match.

Play again: Teams play again. The Receivers become the Senders and the Senders become the Receivers.

3 Receivers Match Design

When the Senders have created their masterpiece, the Receivers attempts to match it. The team works together to try to get the Receivers' design to match that of the Senders. They cannot see the Senders' design, so they must ask questions and the Senders must describe it very well.

Hints

★ **Back to Back.** Instead of using buddy barriers, have pairs work back to back on the floor.
★ **Storing Barriers.** When done with Match Mine, have students fold down their barriers and store them for next time. Use sandwich baggies to store gamepieces. The baggies and gamepieces may be secured with the paper clip.
★ **Sponge Activity.** Teams will finish at different rates. When teams have made a match, have pairs switch roles. The receivers become the senders and vice versa.

RallyTable & RallyRobin

Students take turns as they arrange the pieces (RallyTable), and then describe the pieces (RallyRobin).

Pair Match Mine

Match Mine may also be played in pairs. In the pair version, there is one student on each side of the barrier, rather than two.

Build-What-I-Write

Have the Senders arrange gamepieces, make a design or create a project, whatever it may be. Then, instead of verbally describing it to the Receivers, the Senders describe it in writing as well as they can. The Senders give the Receivers a written description and see how well the Receivers can build what the Senders described.

Draw-What-I-Say

Senders make a drawing. They describe the drawing as well as they can and the Receivers attempt to match the drawing.

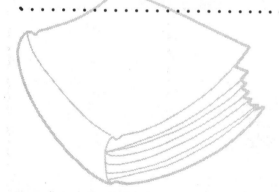

P r i n c i p l e s

Students are strongly interdependent. One pair cannot succeed without the efforts of the other pair.

Students are accountable to their teammates: Senders are accountable for describing the gamepieces; Receivers are accountable for listening and making a match.

To equalize participation, insist on RallyTable while Senders set up their gameboard pieces and RallyTable again when Receivers attempt the match. Insist also on RallyRobin as Senders describe the gamepieces. Also, do Match Mine both ways so students have an equal chance to be Senders and Receivers.

Teams are simultaneously working on Match Mine. Active participation is doubled when pairs rather than teams play Match Mine

Match Mine

Kagans: *Cooperative Learning Structures for Teambuilding*©
Kagan Cooperative Learning • 1(800) WEE CO-OP

Farmyard Fun

Cut out the farm pieces below. **Senders:** Arrange the farm pieces in the boxes below. Describe your arrangement using North, East, South, West. **Receivers:** Match the Senders' arrangement. Switch roles when done.

Cleo the Clown

Cleo can't decide what to
wear. As a team, color his
clothes so you have two
matching sets.
Senders: Dress Cleo then
describe how he is dressed.
Receivers: Match how the
Senders dressed Cleo. Switch
roles when done.

Clothes for Cleo

Color Cleo's clothes so your team has two matching sets. Cut out Cleo's clothes. The **Senders** dress Cleo and the **Receivers** try to match how Cleo is dressed.

Kids for Class Picture

Cut out the students' pictures and names. **Senders:** Take turns placing the students and names on Our Class Picture. Describe your class picture to the Receivers. **Receivers:** Match the Senders' class picture. Switch roles when done.

Chris | Kris | Sean

Kelli | Kelly | Kellie

Joe | Jo | Shawn

Our Class Picture

The **Senders** arrange the students and their names below and the **Receivers** try to match their class picture.

Picture	Picture	Picture
Name	Name	Name
Picture	Picture	Picture
Name	Name	Name
Picture	Picture	Picture
Name	Name	Name

Funny Faces

Cut out the Funny Face pieces. **Senders:** Select different pieces and make a new funny face. Describe your funny face to the Receivers. **Receivers:** Match the Senders' funny face. Switch roles when done.

Hat

| Left Eyebrow | Right Eyebrow |

| Left Ear | Left Eye | Right Eye | Right Ear |

| Left Cheek | Nose & Mouth | Right Cheek |

Neck

Funny Face 1

Cut out the pieces below to design a new funny face.

Funny Face 2

Cut out the pieces below to design a new funny face.

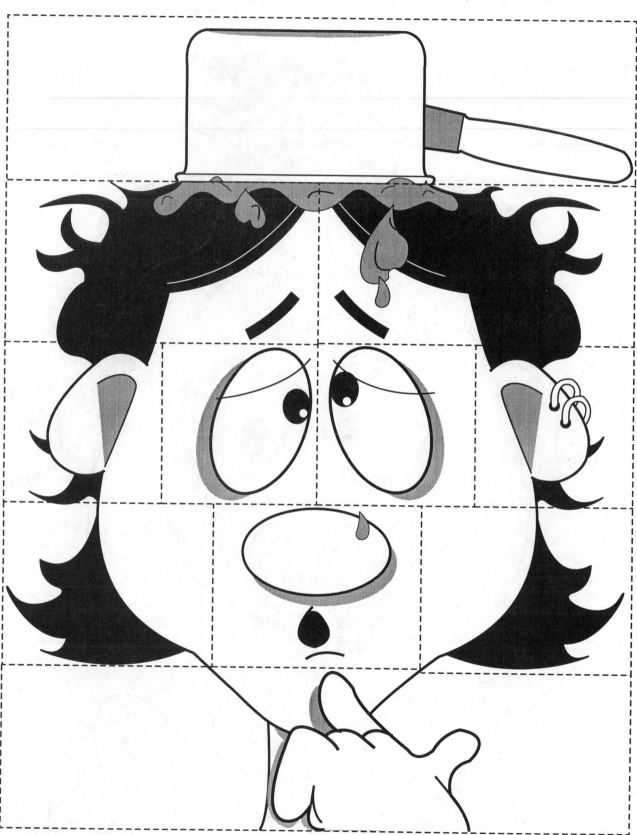

Funny Face 3

Cut out the pieces below to design a new funny face.

Match My Tangram

Each pair gets a set of Tangram pieces. Cut out the shapes. **Senders:** Come up with a design with your Tangram pieces, then describe your design to the Receivers. **Receivers:** Match the Senders' design. Switch roles when done.

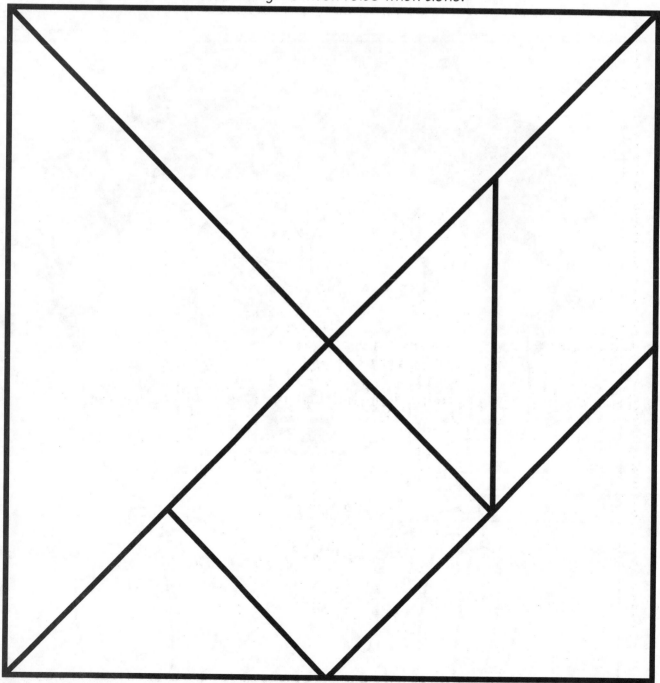

Match My Pythagoras Puzzle

Each pair gets a set of Pythagoras pieces. Cut out the shapes. **Senders:** Come up with a design with your Pythagoras pieces, then describe your design to the Receivers. **Receivers:** Match the Senders' design. Switch roles when done.

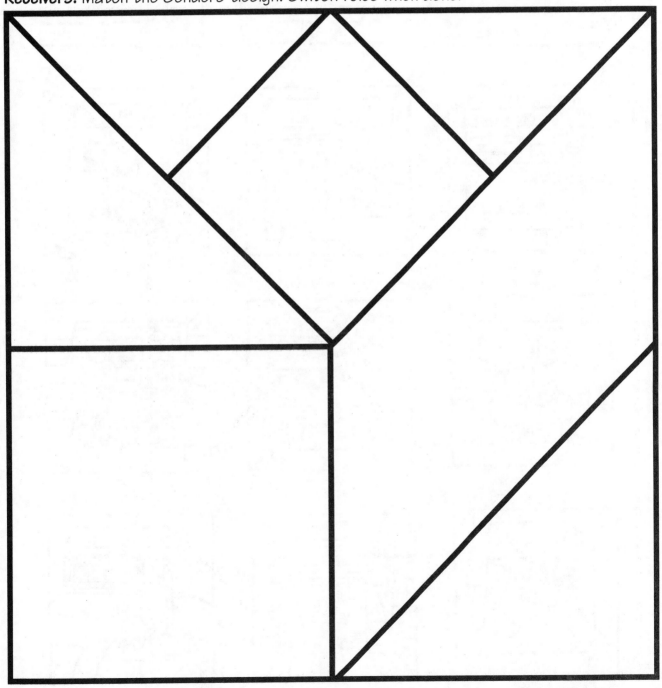

Places for Our Community

Cut out the place pieces below. **Senders:** Place the pieces on Our Community.
Receivers: Match the Senders' community. Switch Roles when done.

Our Community

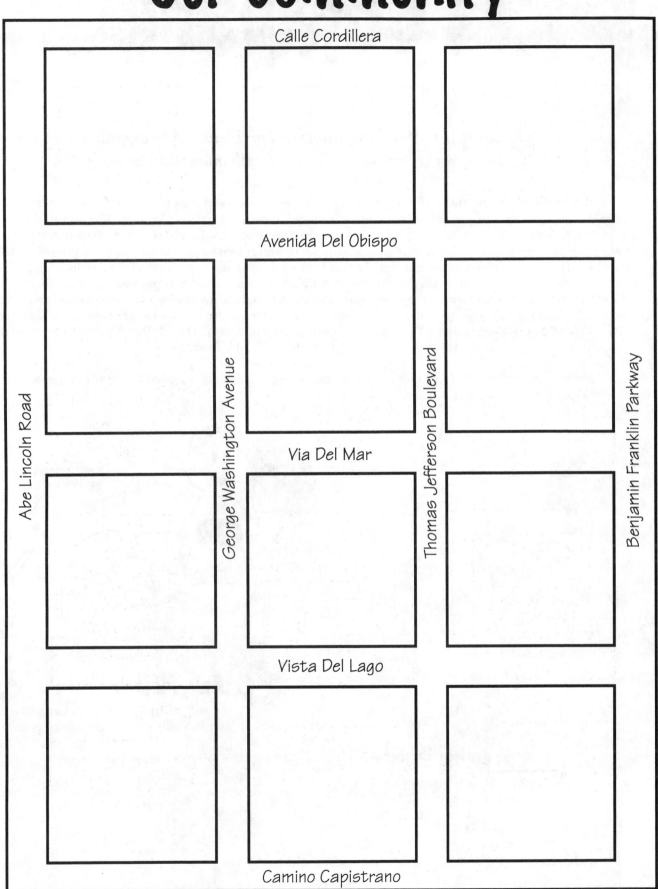

Calle Cordillera

Avenida Del Obispo

Abe Lincoln Road

George Washington Avenue

Via Del Mar

Thomas Jefferson Boulevard

Benjamin Franklin Parkway

Vista Del Lago

Camino Capistrano

Match Mine 75

Pairs Compare

Students work in pairs to list ideas or solutions to a problem; pairs compare their ideas or solutions; then the team works together to come up with more ideas or solutions.

The teacher presents a problem to the class like "Come up with as many words as you can from the letters in the words, 'OUR TEAM.'" Students form pairs and RallyTable ideas, passing their lists back and forth, adding ideas. After the pairs have had some time to generate their own lists, the team unites and pairs compare lists. During Pairs Compare, Student A in pair one states one item from the pair one list, while Student A from pair two either adds the item to the pair two list, or puts a check mark by it, if pair two had also listed the item. Next, Student B from pair one shares a second item from their list while Student B from pair two either checks it off or adds it to the pair two list. Next, Students A and B from pair two, each in turn share items from their list while their counterparts in pair one either add or check off the items. The Pairs Compare step continues until both pairs have shared all items and both pairs have identical lists. In the last step of this structure, the Team Challenge, all four teammates work together to see if they can come up with even more ideas to add to the lists. A's in each pair record the first new item on their respective lists, B's the next and so on, in a RallyTable format.

Pairs Compare is a strong structure for developing team synergy because teams are challenged to come up with new ideas based on the work of the pairs.

2 RallyTable

In pairs, students record their ideas passing the list back and forth, each adding an idea in turn.

1 Teacher Presents Problem

The teacher presents to the class a problem on which students can come up with a list of ideas. *"List some positive statements you can use to appreciate a teammate."*

4 Team Challenge

The challenge is for teams to come with new ideas that neither pair alone had generated. During this step, the two lists continue to be passed back and forth in a RallyTable within pairs. A's and B's in each pair alternate recording the new ideas generated by the team, no matter who came up with the ideas.

3 Pairs Compare

When pairs have a list of ideas, the pairs unite to compare the ideas they each came up with. If the other pair came up with the same idea, a check is placed next to the idea. If the other pair came up with a different idea, that idea is added to each pair's list. When pairs are done comparing lists, both pairs have identical lists.

Hint

★ **Uneven Teams.** If there are one, two or three students left over that don't fit into a group of four, send them each to a different team of four to form up to three teams of five. During pair work, in the teams of five, a pair and a triad are formed.

Problem Solving

Instead of using Pairs Compare to generate a list, use Pairs Compare for problem solving. Select problems which may be solved in a variety of ways, or may have a number of possible answers or ideas. Pairs compare their answers in turn and the team challenge is to come up with solutions to the problem that neither pair alone had thought of.

Category Frames

When pairs record their ideas, let them use a graphic organizer such as a Venn diagram, a PMI frame, or a Two-by-Two matrix.

Two-by-Two Matrix

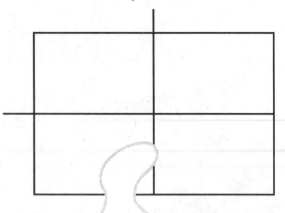

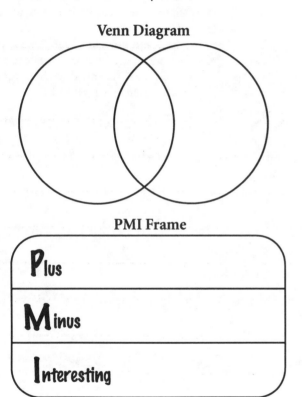

Venn Diagram

PMI Frame

Plus

Minus

Interesting

Principles

 Partners are interdependent during the pair work; teammates are interdependent during the team work.

 RallyTable throughout the structure makes individuals accountable to their partner for coming up with and recording ideas.

 RallyTable ensures equal participation.

 At any one moment, half the class is active, recording ideas during all steps of this structure.

Pairs Compare

Kagans: *Cooperative Learning Structures for Teambuilding©*
Kagan Cooperative Learning • 1(800) WEE CO-OP

Qualities of a Good Teammember

In pairs, take turns listing all the qualities of a good team-member. Compare your list with another pair and see if you came up with the same answers. Then, as a team of four, see if you can all come up with new ideas.

_____   _____

_____   _____

_____   _____

_____   _____

_____   _____

_____   _____

_____   _____

_____   _____

_____   _____

_____   _____

_____   _____

_____   _____

Are these qualities that you have? What can you work on?

A Good Cooperative Learning Team

In pairs, take turns listing what you can do to make working together better. Compare your list with another pair and see if you came up with the same answers. Then, as a team of four, see if you can all come up with new ideas.

_____ _____

_____ _____

_____ _____

_____ _____

_____ _____

_____ _____

_____ _____

_____ _____

_____ _____

_____ _____

_____ _____

_____ _____

Wish Upon a Star

In pairs, take turns listing all the things you wish you could do, have, or be. Compare your list with another pair and see if you came up with the same wishes. Then, as a team of four, see if you can all come up with new wishes.

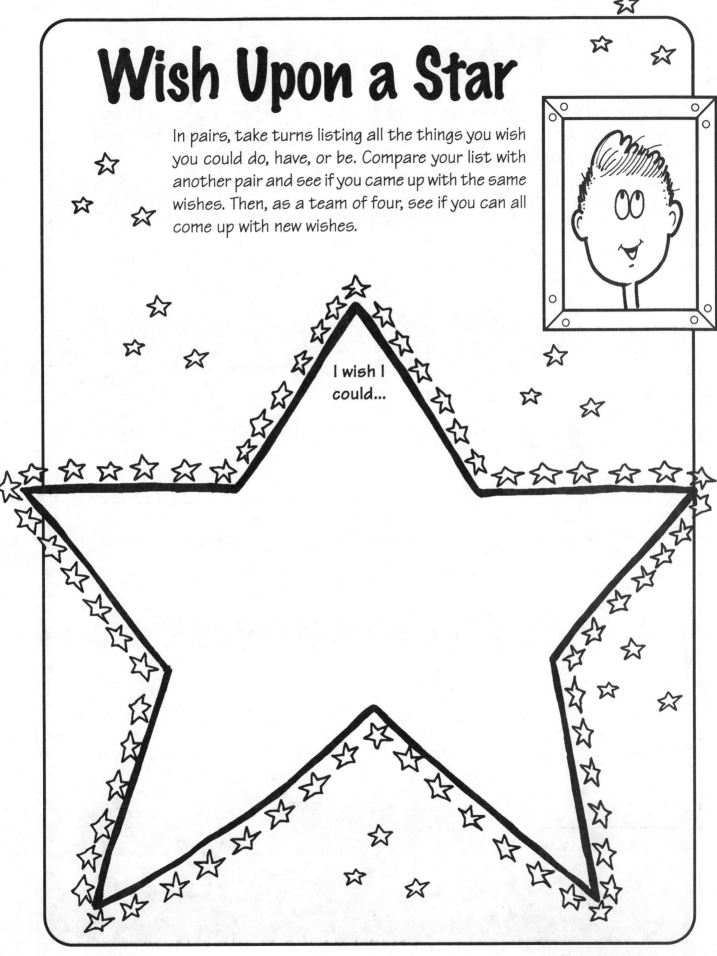

I wish I could...

I Wanna Visit...

In pairs, take turns listing places you'd like to visit. Compare your list with another pair and see if you came up with the same places. Then, as a team of four, see if you can all come up with new places.

Road Map

My Favorite Music

In pairs, take turns listing your favorite musical groups or musicians. Compare your list with another pair and see if you came up with the same groups. Then, as a team of four, see if you can all come up with new groups.

_____

_____

_____   _____

_____   _____

_____   _____

_____   _____

_____   _____

_____   _____

_____   _____

_____   _____

_____   _____

_____   _____

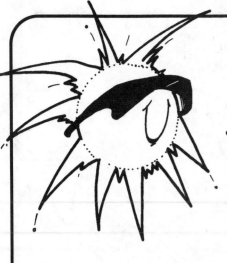

My Favorite Summer Activities

In pairs, list all your favorite summer activities. Compare your list with another pair. Then, as a team of four, see if you can all come up with new activities.

_____   _____   _____

_____   _____   _____

_____   _____   _____

_____   _____   _____

_____   _____   _____

My Favorite Fall Activities

In pairs, list all your favorite fall activities. Compare your list with another pair. Then, as a team of four, see if you can all come up with new activities.

_____   _____   _____

_____   _____   _____

_____   _____   _____

_____   _____   _____

My Favorite Spring Activities

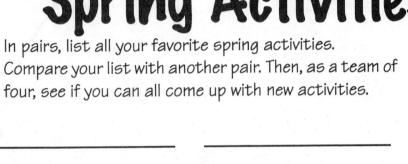

In pairs, list all your favorite spring activities. Compare your list with another pair. Then, as a team of four, see if you can all come up with new activities.

_____ _____ _____

_____ _____ _____

_____ _____ _____

_____ _____ _____

_____ _____ _____

My Favorite Winter Activities

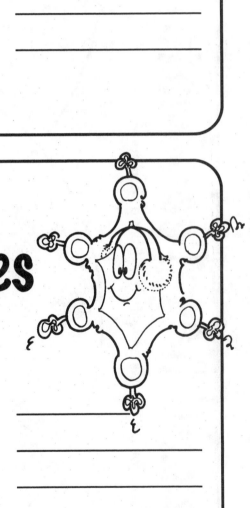

In pairs, list all your favorite winter activities. Compare your list with another pair. Then, as a team of four, see if you can all come up with new activities.

_____ _____ _____

_____ _____ _____

_____ _____ _____

_____ _____ _____

_____ _____ _____

Me and My Teammate

Find out how you are similar and different from a teammate.

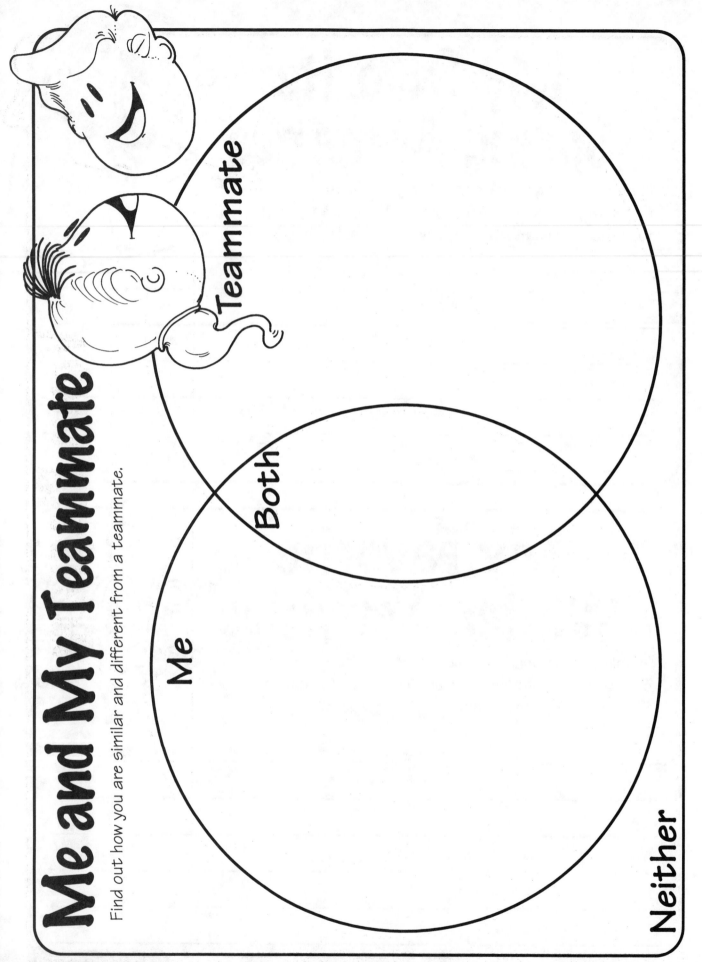

Teammate

Both

Me

Neither

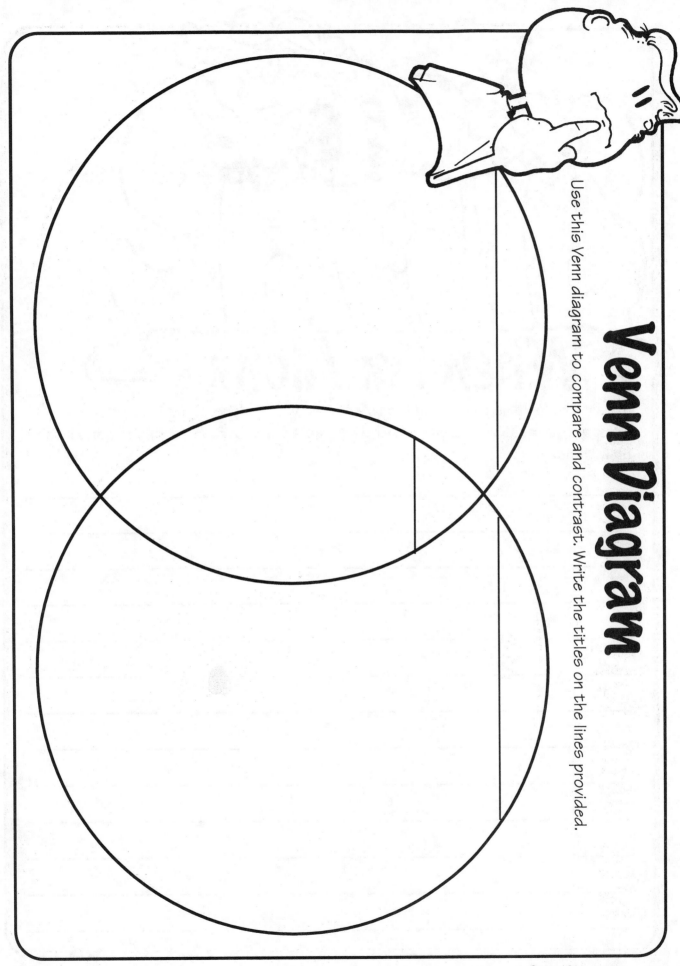

Venn Diagram

Use this Venn diagram to compare and contrast. Write the titles on the lines provided.

When I'm Alone

In pairs, list all the things you like to do when you're alone.
Compare your list with another pair. Then, as a team of four, see if you can all come up with new ideas.

My Favorite TV Shows

In pairs, list your favorite TV shows. Compare your list with another pair.
Then, as a team of four, see if you can all come up with new shows.

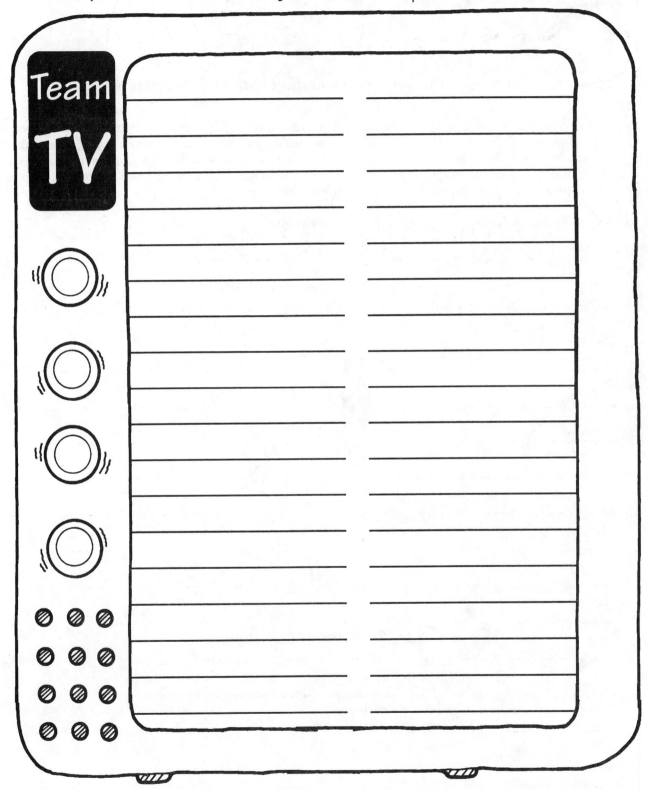

Team
TV

RoundRobin

Students take turns verbally sharing information with their teammates.

RoundRobin is a simple turn allocation structure. The teacher announces a topic and each student in turn shares something with teammates. RoundRobin is flexible. It can be used for a variety of teambuilding activities, depending on the content. RoundRobin may be used for getting acquainted activities, "Share with the team your favorite thing to do after school;" it may be used for synergy, "Come up with ideas for team reunions;" it may be used for students to appreciate different perspectives, "How do you feel about affirmative action?"

RoundRobin increases active participation by all teammates and promotes active listening.

1 Teacher Announces Topic

Announce the topic on which students are to share something with the team. *"In your teams, RoundRobin what you did this weekend. Start with Student Two."*

② Students Take Turns Talking

In turn, each student shares information with the team.

Hints

★ **Polite Listening.** Make sure to mention that no one is to speak out of turn. When it is not their turn, teammates are to practice "polite listening."

★ **Right to Pass.** Students may need some more time to think about what they want to say or how they want to present it. Rather than holding up the team, students can "pass" one round.

★ **Many Rounds.** Select topics that students can make meaningful contributions for several rounds.

Timed-RoundRobin
If the topic is sharing an opinion on something which may be time consuming, assign the role of timekeeper. Each student gets one minute for their turn.

RallyRobin
RallyRobin is RoundRobin in pairs. In RallyRobin, students take turns with their partner making a contribution. It is called RallyRobin because students go back and forth like in a ping pong rally.

Turn Toss
Each time they share, students toss a ball or crumpled piece of paper to another teammate. It is then that teammate's turn. "No toss backs" ensures one pair does not take all the turns.

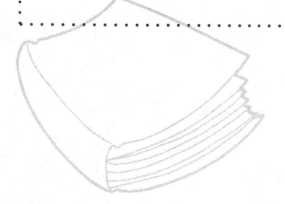

Principles

An idea shared by a teammate may help trigger a new idea.

Each student is accountable to the team for sharing information.

Students participate roughly equally as each student makes a contribution in turn. The no toss back rule in Turn Toss helps equalize participation.

In RoundRobin, one quarter of the class is participating at any one time; one half in RallyRobin.

RoundRobin

Kagans: *Cooperative Learning Structures for Teambuilding*©
Kagan Cooperative Learning • 1(800) WEE CO-OP

My Birth Certificate

Fill in your Birth Certificate and share about yourself with your teammates.

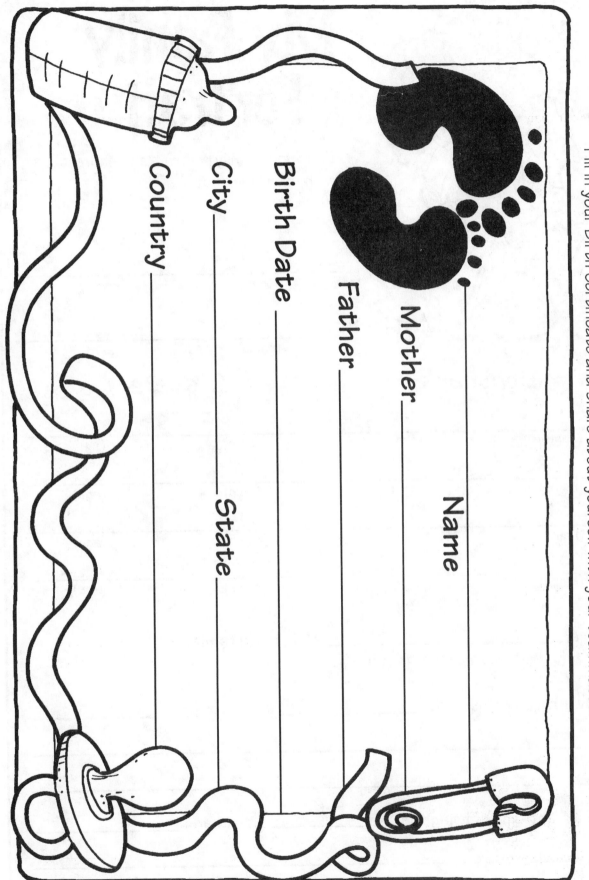

Name _____

Mother _____

Father _____

Birth Date _____

City _____ State _____

Country _____

My Family Portrait

Fill in your family portrait and share it with your teammates.

Father_____

                (name)   (age)

Mother_____

                (name)   (age)

Brothers		Sisters	
(name)	(age)	(name)	(age)
(name)	(age)	(name)	(age)
(name)	(age)	(name)	(age)
(name)	(age)	(name)	(age)

I am the_____ child in my family.

        (oldest, youngest, middle, only)

The advantages of being the _____ child are: _____

_____

_____

The disadvantages of being the _____ child are: _____

_____

_____

All About Me Book

Have students make a book about themselves and share it with their teammates.

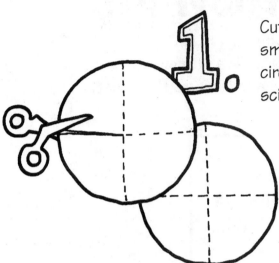

Cut two 11" circles out of construction paper (use smaller circles for a smaller book). Fold both circles in quarters and then unfold them. With scissors, cut along one fold line to the center.

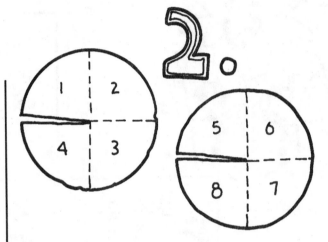

Number the first circle from 1 to 4 clockwise from the slit and the second circle 5 to 8 clockwise from the slit.

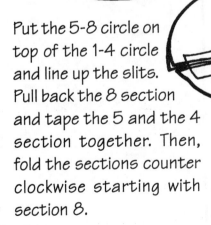

Put the 5-8 circle on top of the 1-4 circle and line up the slits. Pull back the 8 section and tape the 5 and the 4 section together. Then, fold the sections counter clockwise starting with section 8.

All About Me!

Keep folding until you have the book. Have students write and illustrate their books and share it with teammates.

School Days Question Die

Cut out the pattern and fold it into a die. Tape the die together. Student 1 rolls the die and answers the question. Then, Student 2 rolls the die and answers the question. Keep taking turns for several rounds.

If I were the teacher, I'd...

The best thing I've done so far this year is...

The hardest part of school is...

A new subject we should study is...

The easiest part of school is...

The best part of school is...

Blackout

Student One picks a square and reads it aloud to teammates. He or she calls on a teammate to answer the statement. After the teammate answers, the square is covered up with a marker or bean. Student two reads a different square. The game is complete when all squares are blacked out.

Your Birthplace or Hometown	Your Best Memories	Places You've Lived	Schools You've Attended
Your Dreams or Goals	Your Favorite School Subject	Awards You've Received	Vacations You've Taken
Your Favorite Music	Your Favorite Color	Summer Camps You've Attended	Your Favorite Dinner
Your Hobbies	Sports You Play	Your Nickname	Your Favorite Dessert

Closest to Me

Make a map of the people who are close to you. Place the name in relation to how close the people are to you in real life. Draw circles around the names and lines connecting to "ME." Share your map with teammates.

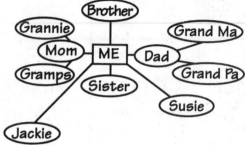

Magic Stars

These Magic Stars turn you into someone or something else. Cut out the magic stars, place them face down on your desks and shuffle them. Student One picks one star, shares with the team who or what he or she would be and why. After Student One shares, the star is shuffled with the rest of the stars. Student Two picks a star and shares.

Murder Mystery

Cut out the clue cards. Hand them out in your team clockwise so Student 1 gets card 1, Student 2, card 2... Read 4 clues then stop to figure out 1. Who killed Mr. Garcia? 2. What time was he murdered? 3. What was the murder weapon? 4. Why was he murdered? If you can not figure out the answers, read the next 4 clues, then stop and figure out the answers. Continue until you've read all clues, then check your answer against the correct answer.

1. When he was discovered, Mr. Garcia had a bullet hole in his arm and a dagger wound in his back.

8. Mr. Garcia had destroyed Mr. Dyer's pizza business by opening a better restaurant next door.

2. Mr. Dyer shot an intruder in his apartment building at midnight.

9. The door man saw Mr. Garcia's wife go to Mr. Anderson's apartment at 11:30 p.m.

3. The door man told police that he saw Mr. Garcia at 12:15 a.m.

10. The door man said that Mr. Garcia's wife frequently left the building with Mr. Anderson.

4. The bullet taken from Mr. Garcia's arm matched the rifle owned by Mr. Dyer.

11. Mr. Garcia's body was found in the playground.

5. Only one bullet had been fired from Mr. Dyer's rifle.

12. Mr. Garcia's body was found at 1:30 a.m.

6. Mr. Garcia's arm was bleeding slightly when the door man saw him, but he did not seem too badly hurt.

13. According to the medical expert, Mr. Garcia had been dead for one hour when his body was found.

7. A dagger found in Miss Slater's front yard had Mr. Anderson's fingerprints on it.

14. The door man saw Mr. Garcia go to Mr. Anderson's room at 12:25 a.m.

Murder Mystery

15. The door man went off duty at 12:30 a.m.

16. The medical expert determined that Mr. Garcia's body had been dragged a long distance.

17. Miss Slater saw Mr. Garcia go to Mr. Dyer's apartment building at 11:55 p.m.

18. Mr. Garcia's wife disappeared after the murder.

19. Police were unable to locate Mr. Anderson after the murder.

20. The police could not locate Mr. Dyer after the murder for questioning.

21. Miss Slater was spotted in the apartment lobby by the door man when he went off duty.

22. Mr. Dyer had told Mr. Garcia that he was going to kill him.

23. Miss Slater often followed Mr. Garcia.

24. Miss Slater said that nobody left the apartment building between 12:25 a.m. and 12:45 a.m.

25. The medical expert determined the blood stains on the carpet outside Mr. Dyer's apartment belonged to Mr. Garcia.

Answer: Mr. Dyer shot Mr. Garcia in the arm with his rifle, but the shot did not kill Mr. Garcia. Mr. Garcia went to Mr. Anderson's apartment where Mr. Anderson killed Mr. Garcia with a dagger in the back at 12:30 a.m. The Motive: Mr. Anderson was in love with Mr. Garcia's wife.

RoundTable

In turn, each student makes a contribution to the team's project that is passed around the table.

RoundTable is a fun and easy turn allocation structure. Whether it be a list, a story, or a project, students literally pass it around the table, thus the name RoundTable. When it is their turn, each student makes a contribution to whatever the team is working on. If teams are working on a list of reasons why they enjoy working with their teammates, a pen and paper are passed around the table, stopping at each student as they add their reason to the list. If teams are writing a team story, they pass around the paper and each student adds the next sentence. If it is a team collage, each student in turn glues on the next piece.

RoundTable is good for mutual support and developing synergy in teams. Teammates all work on the same project and build on each others' contribution.

1 Teacher Gives Directions

Announce the topic students are to work on. *"In teams, come up with a list of favorite foods in alphabetical order: Apple pie, Banana Nut Bread, Chocolate... Pass a sheet of paper and a pen around the table clockwise. When the paper comes to you, write down one of your favorite foods starting with the next letter."*

② Students Take Turns

In turn, each student makes their contribution.

Timed-RoundTable

If the task is complex, assign the role of timekeeper. Each student gets one minute for their turn.

RallyTable

RallyTable is RoundTable in pairs. In RallyTable, students take turns with their partner making a contribution. It is called RallyTable because students go back and forth like a ping pong rally.

Simultaneous RoundTable

Simultaneous RoundTable increases active participation and the number of responses. Instead of one paper and one pen per team, in Simultaneous RoundTable there are four papers and four pens. Each teammate makes a contribution then passes the paper to the teammate on the left. Each teammate simultaneously contributes.

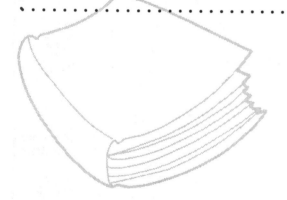

Principles

Students depend on each other to contribute to make the project go around the table.

Each student is accountable to the team for making a contribution. Increase individual accountability by having students write with different colored pens or markers.

Students participate roughly equally as each student makes a contribution in turn.

In RoundTable, one quarter of the class is participating at any one time. In a RallyTable, one half are active at any moment. In Simultaneous RoundTable all are active at once.

RoundTable

Kagans: *Cooperative Learning Structures for Teambuilding*©
Kagan Cooperative Learning • 1(800) WEE CO-OP

School and Baseball are...

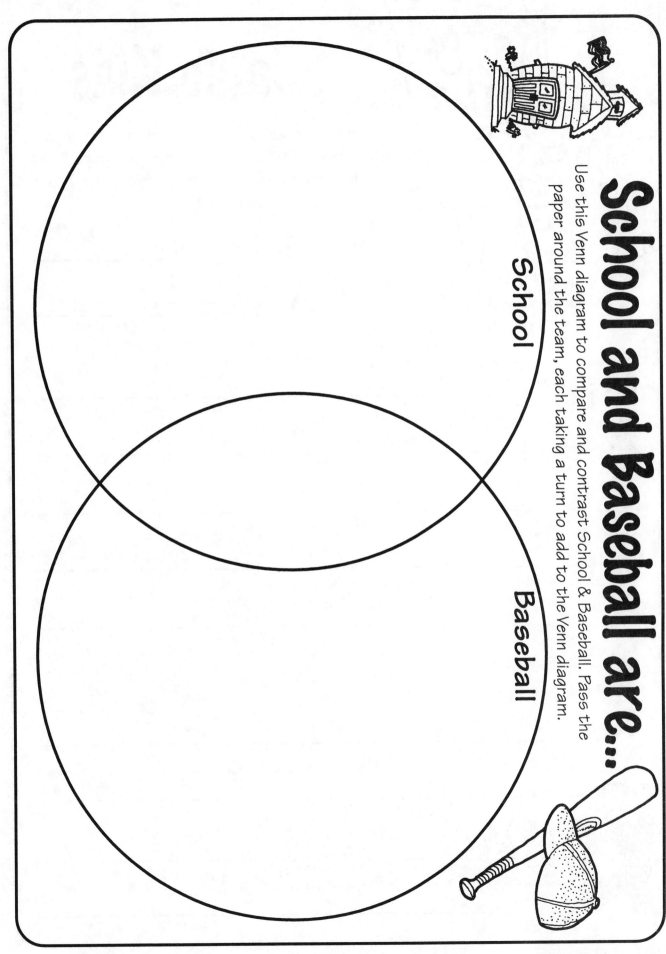

Use this Venn diagram to compare and contrast School & Baseball. Pass the paper around the team, each taking a turn to add to the Venn diagram.

School

Baseball

Magic Kids

In teams, take turns writing a sentence about your team beginning with the first letters of "Magic Kids." You must check to make sure everyone agrees before you can write your sentence.

Example: **M** ost of us like chocolate. _____

A ll of us help each other out! _____

M _____

A _____

G _____

I _____

C _____

K _____

I _____

D _____

S _____

A Good Look

Fold this page on the fold line. Take a good look at the picture. In 1 minute you will take turns recording everything you can remember about the picture. When done, unfold the page and check your observations with the picture.

(fold)

Recording Sheet

_____ _____
_____ _____
_____ _____
_____ _____
_____ _____
_____ _____
_____ _____
_____ _____
_____ _____
_____ _____

Build the Picture

Carefully cut out the picture along the lines. Place the boxes face down on the table and shuffle them. Pass out the boxes so everyone has an equal number. Take turns laying out the picture. No one can touch anyone else's picture box.

Our Team Likes

Student 1 says: "I like to rollerblade. Who likes to rollerblade?" If no one else likes to, "rollerblade" is written in box 1, If everyone likes to rollerblade, "rollerblade" is written in the "All" circle. Take turns saying "Who likes..." and recording it.

who likes...

1

2

All

3

Team Barnyard Scene

Each student gets one picture. Add to the picture. Pass pictures clockwise every 15 seconds. Continue adding to the new picture when it comes to you.

Team Squiggle Art

Each student gets one picture and a different color marker or crayon. Add to the squiggle art until the teacher calls "switch!" Then pass the picture clockwise and continue adding to the new picture.

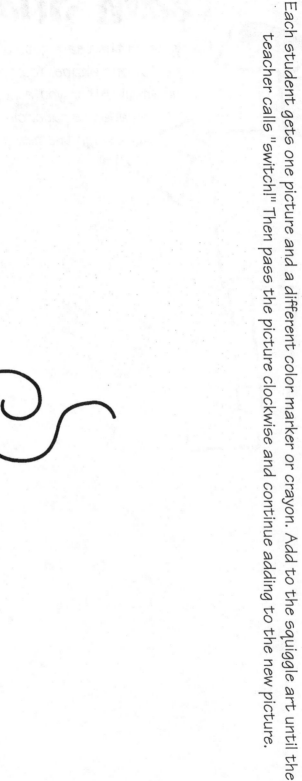

Simultaneous RoundTable

Team Shape Picture

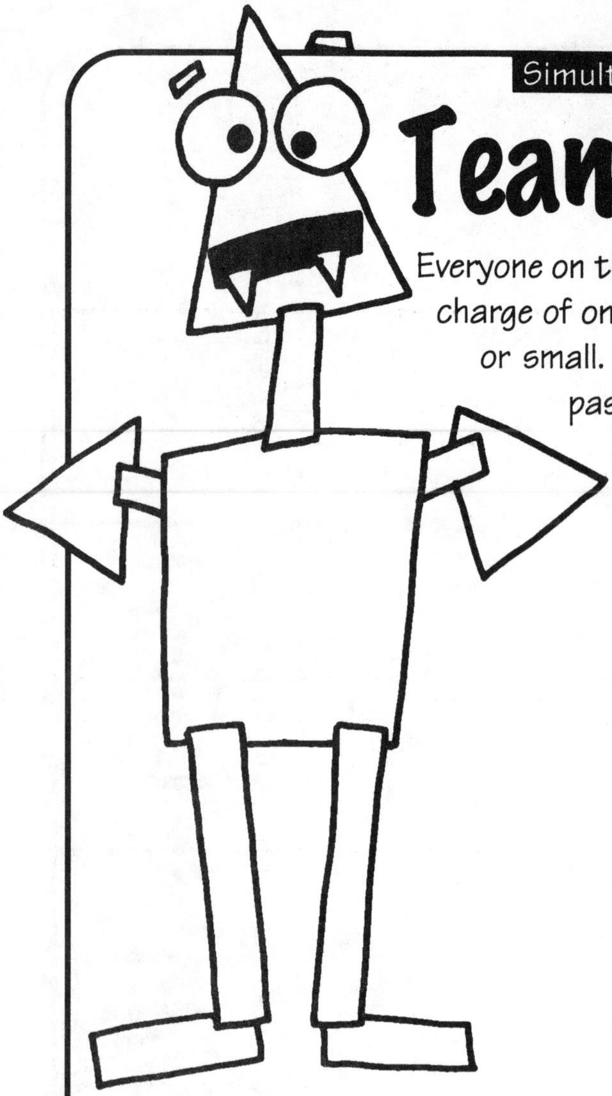

Everyone on the team gets one Team Shape Picture. You are in charge of one shape. You can draw your shape large, medium or small. After you add your shape to the team picture, pass the paper clockwise. Continue adding your shape when the new picture comes to you.

- **Student 1 - Triangles**
- **Student 2 - Squares**
- **Student 3 - Circles**
- **Student 4 - Rectangles**

Shape Creation

Everyone on the team gets 1 large sheet of white paper, 1 glue stick, and the shapes below. Color your shapes, then cut them out. Glue down your shape, then pass your sheet clockwise. Add a new shape when the new picture comes to you. What can your team create?

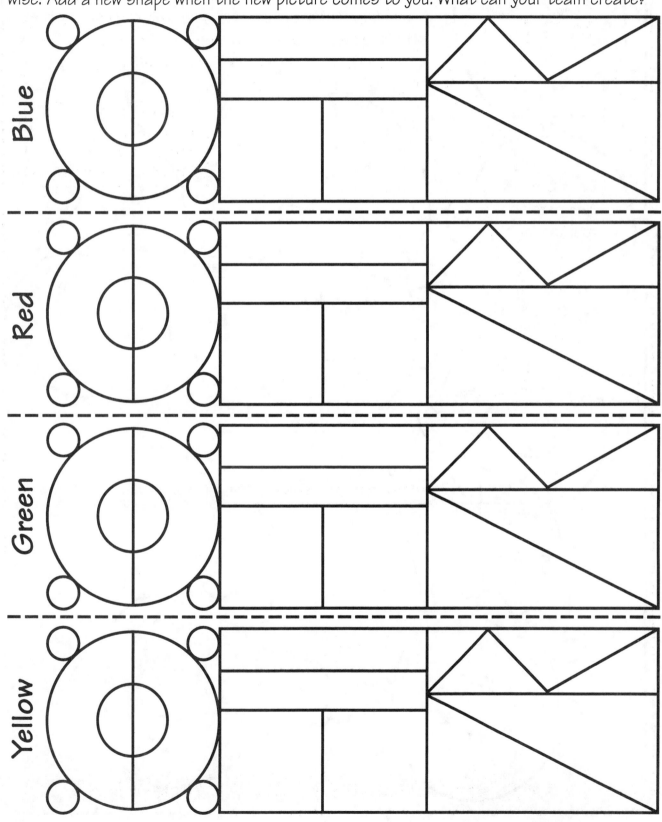

Blue

Red

Green

Yellow

Build a Clown

Teacher Directions. Give each student one sheet. Lead the class through the steps of drawing a clown. Have them pass papers clockwise after each step.

Step 1
Draw a circle.

Pass Papers

Step 2
Add ears to your circle.

Pass Papers

Step 3
Now add a nose.

Pass Papers

Step 4
Add a hat.

Pass Papers

Step 5
Add eyes above the nose.

Pass Papers

Step 6
Add a smile.

Pass Papers

Step 7
Add hair and details.

Making 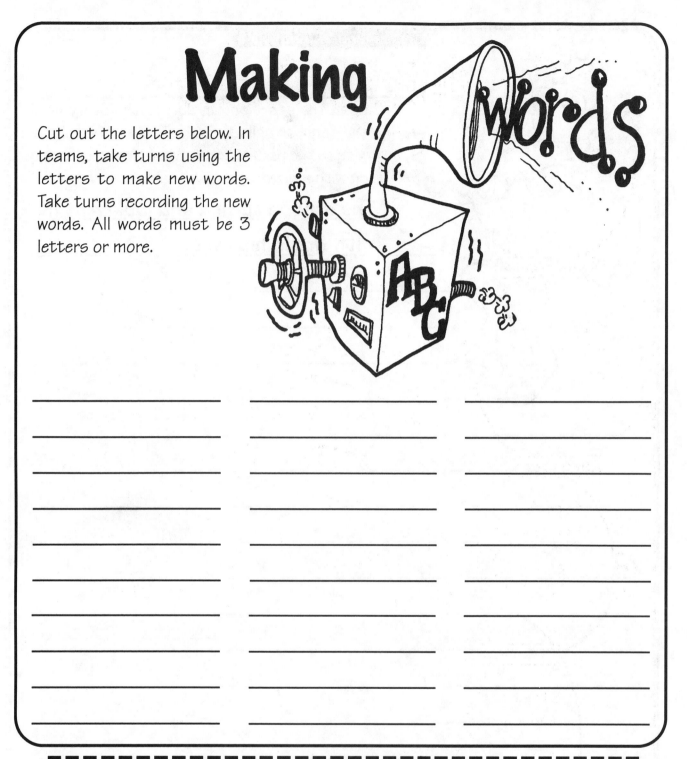words

Cut out the letters below. In teams, take turns using the letters to make new words. Take turns recording the new words. All words must be 3 letters or more.

_____   _____   _____
_____   _____   _____
_____   _____   _____
_____   _____   _____
_____   _____   _____
_____   _____   _____
_____   _____   _____
_____   _____   _____

O U R T E A M I S

F A N T A S T I C

Simultaneous RoundTable

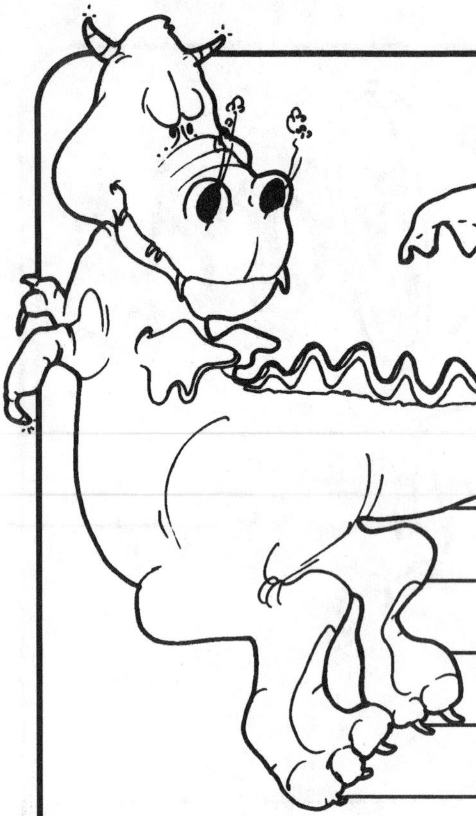

Title

Read the story so far, add to the story until the teacher calls time. Pass the story clockwise to the next student. When time is up, come up with a good title as a team.

The dragon turned and looked at me with fire in his eyes.

Title

Read the story so far, add to the story until the teacher calls time. Pass the story clockwise to the next student. When time is up, come up with a good title as a team.

"Aha, these are the professor's fingerprints," said the detective.

_____

_____

_____

_____

_____

_____

_____

_____

_____

_____

_____

_____

_____

_____

_____

_____

_____

_____

Title

Read the story so far, add to the story until the teacher calls time. Pass the story clockwise to the next student. When time is up, come up with a good title as a team.

He fired his Colt .45 in the air and shouted, "Stop right there!"

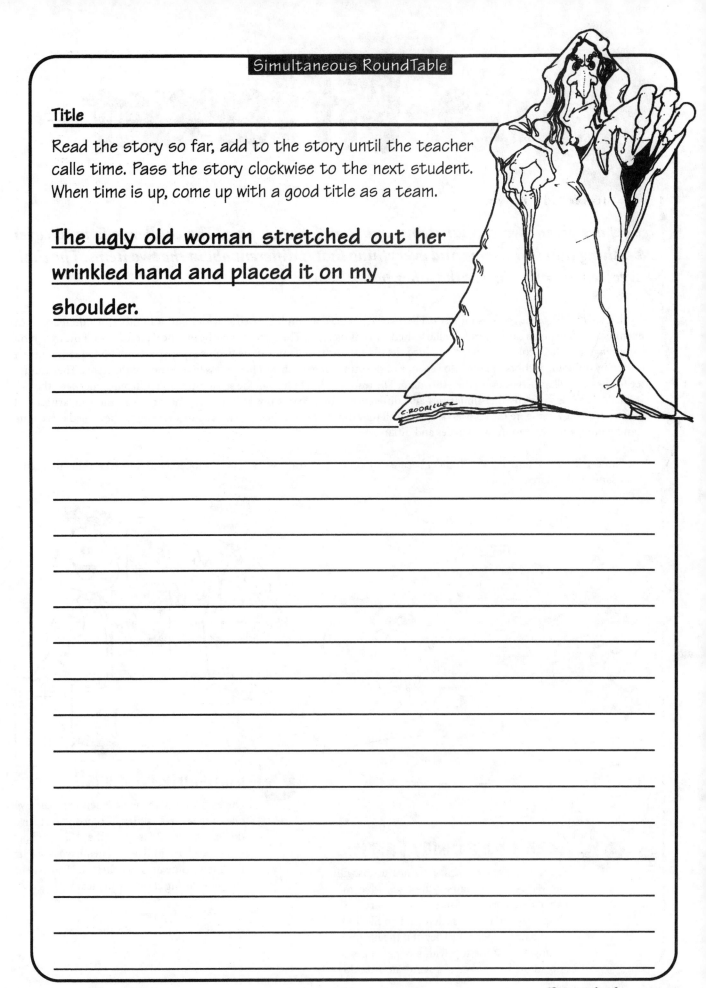

Title _____

Read the story so far, add to the story until the teacher calls time. Pass the story clockwise to the next student. When time is up, come up with a good title as a team.

The ugly old woman stretched out her

wrinkled hand and placed it on my

shoulder.

_____

_____

_____

_____

_____

_____

_____

_____

_____

_____

_____

_____

_____

_____

_____

_____

_____

_____

RoundTable 119

Same-Different

Teams are given two similar items, one item for each pair. The challenge is to uncover everything that is the same and everything that is different about the two items. The challenge: Neither pair can see the other pair's item.

Each pair on the team receives an item. The two items have a number of similarities and a number of differences. For example, the two items can be carefully illustrated pairs of pictures. The pictures may be identical pictures with the exception of missing, modified, colored, moved or added details. Or, the two items can be two newspaper articles on the same subject written by different authors or even two versions of the same song. Each pair has access to only one of the items. They cannot see (or hear, smell, touch or taste) the other item. The team's task is to find all the similarities and differences between the two items. A recorder records the similarities and differences. After teams think they have uncovered all the similarities and differences, they compare the items to see how well they did. The team checks to make sure everything they listed is accurate and continues to find more similarities and differences.

Same-Different is a strong teambuilder because students must really work carefully together to find everything that is the same and different.

1 Teams Build Buddy Barriers

For most Same-Different activities, teams will need a barrier so pairs cannot see what the other pair has. File folder barriers are very simple to build. Give each team two file folders and one paper clip. They clip the file folders together at the top with a paper clip and spread the base to make a stand-alone buddy barrier.

2 Distribute Materials

Once students have their barriers in place, have one of the Pair A students come up to receive the Pair A item. Make sure they do not show what they have to Pair B. Then have one Pair B student come up and collect the Pair B item and a recording sheet for the team.

120

4 Pairs Compare Pictures

When the team has uncovered all the similarities and differences or can't find any more, they compare their pictures. They go over all the similarities and differences they recorded and make sure they are accurate. Then, they continue to find more similarities and differences.

3 Students Discover Similarities & Differences

The team works together to discover everything that is the same and everything that is different about the two items. RoundTable is used to record the similarities and differences.

Hints

★ **Different Materials.** Same-Different can be played with a number of materials. Try Same-Different with pictures, articles, advertisements, foods, soft drink cans, music, rocks, plants, materials, books, problems, films.

★ **Reflection Time.** Interrupt students after a few minutes of playing. Ask them to reflect on what roles and strategies they are using, and what is being effective and what is not working.

★ **Storing the Barriers.** When done with Same-Different, students fold down their barriers and store them for next time. If you are doing Same-Different with pictures or articles, use the paper clip to secure the materials inside the folded folders.

Pair Same-Different

Same-Different can be played in pairs. In this case, there is one student on each side of the buddy barrier rather than two.

Class Same-Different

For younger students, try Same-Different with the entire class. Half the class has access to one item and the other half to another item. The whole class works together to find similarities and differences.

Class Rewards

Offer different rewards at different point levels. Teams earn one point for every similarity they find and two points for every difference. Teams sum their points and work toward the class goal.

No Barrier

For younger students, give each team two items. Their task is to find the similarities and differences as a team. No barrier is used.

Between-Team Competition

Teams are given a limited amount of time and must find as many similarities and differences as possible. The team with the most points wins. Their prize is to share with the class their method of working so efficiently.

Memory Only

Students are given two or three minutes to look at their object, then must set it out of sight. Teams work together to see how many similarities and differences they can discover from memory. Alternatively, students can look at an answer key for one minute, and may try to remember as many similarities and differences as they can.

Writing Only

Pairs write their description of the item as well as possible. Then, they give the other pair on the team a copy of what they wrote. The pairs then use the other pairs' written description of the item to find as many similarities and differences as they can.

Passing Notes

Pairs are not allowed to speak. They pass notes up and back to discover what is same and different in their teams.

Principles

Students are strongly interdependent. One pair cannot succeed without the efforts of the other pair.

Students are accountable to their teammates for their participation. Teams can be held accountable by collecting their recording sheets.

To equalize participation, use a RoundTable to find and record the next similarity or difference..

Teams are simultaneously working on Same-Different.

Same-Different

Same

Different

Same	Different
1. _____	1. _____
2. _____	2. _____
3. _____	3. _____
4. _____	4. _____
5. _____	5. _____
6. _____	6. _____
7. _____	7. _____
8. _____	8. _____
9. _____	9. _____
10. _____	10. _____
11. _____	11. _____
12. _____	12. _____
13. _____	13. _____
14. _____	14. _____
15. _____	15. _____
16. _____	16. _____
17. _____	17. _____
18. _____	18. _____
19. _____	19. _____
20. _____	20. _____

Same-Different   123

Outer Space

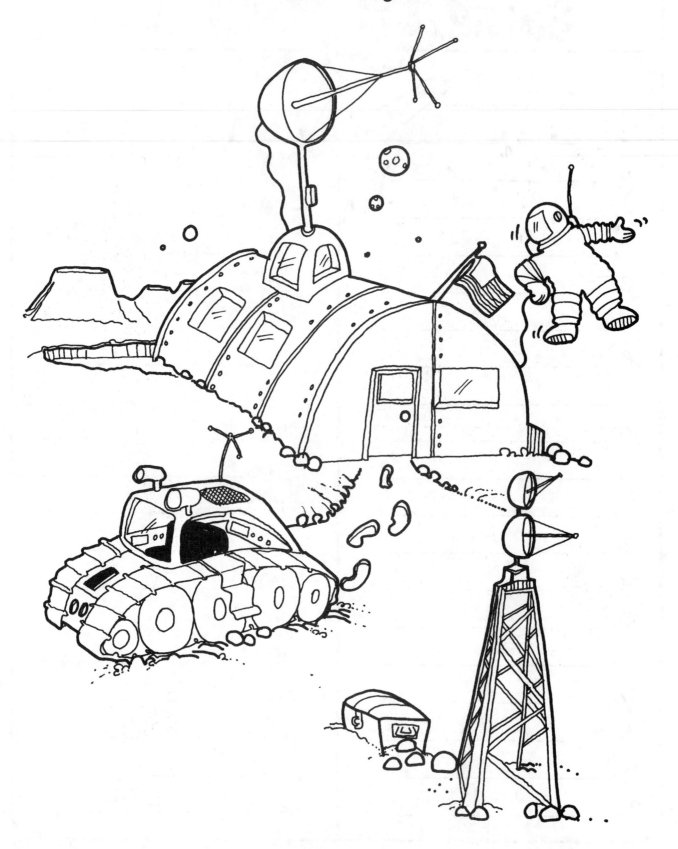

Outer Space

Space
Station

Outer Space Key

1. Location of planets
2. Number of planets
3. Location of footsteps
4. Number of chests
5. Color of space mobile's tires
6. Bolts on space station
7. Antenna on space mobile
8. Windows on space station
9. Number of astronauts
10. Craters under astronaut
11. Color of astronaut's suit
12. Color of space station
13. Flag on space station
14. Rocks behind space mobile
15. Sign on space station

Pat the Raccoon Key

1. One is a boy, the other a girl

2. Mouth is open

3. Bow

4. Hair

5. Eyebrows

6. Eyelashes

7. Shirt/blouse style

8. Buttons

9. Position of arms

10. Position of legs

11. Short style

12. Shoe style

13. Shoelaces

Same-Different   127

Pat the Raccoon

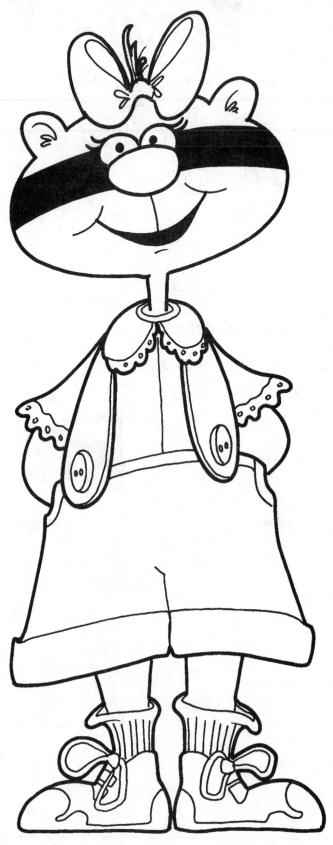

Pat the Raccoon

Super Hero

Super Hero

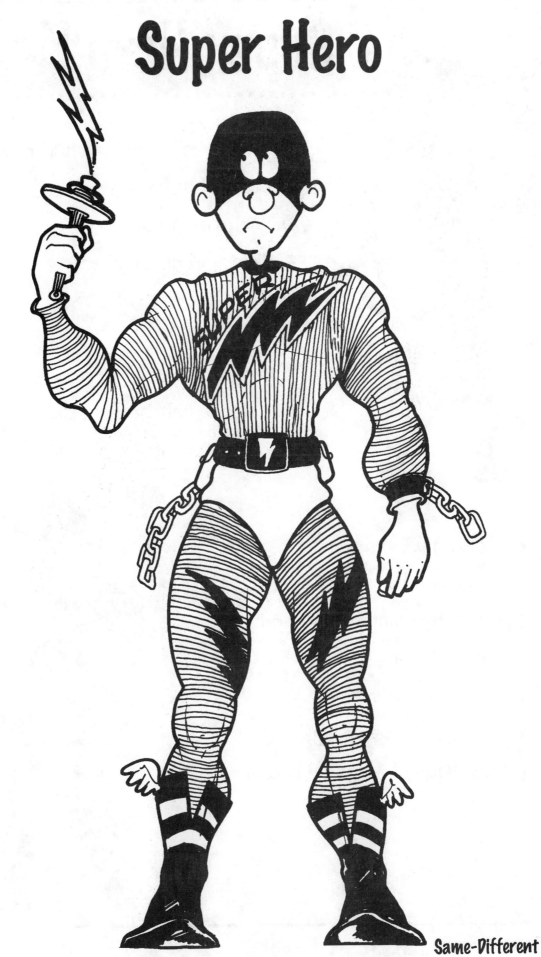

Super Hero Key

1. Number of bolts in bolt thrower
2. Color of mask
3. Wings on mask
4. Color of bolt on chest
5. Cape
6. Color of collar
7. Length of neck
8. Color of belt and buckle

9. Bolt on belt buckle
10. Chain on belt
11. Links in chain on left hand
12. Smile/frown
13. Direction of eyes
14. Color of bolts on legs
15. Location of wings on boots

Pencil

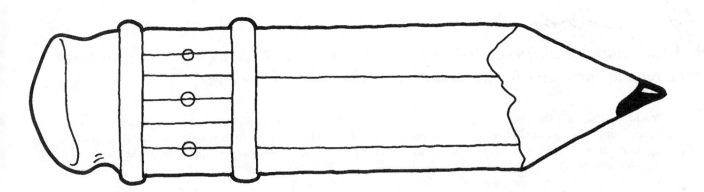

Crayon

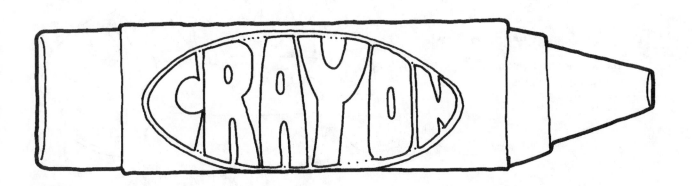

Same-Different   133

Team Interview

Each teammate experiences both sides of the interview coin: They are interviewed by three teammates at once, and also act three times in the role of interviewer.

The teacher introduces a topic for the Team Interview. "If you could be rich and famous for some accomplishment, what would it be?" In each team, one student stands up. For one minute (or whatever time limit is set) that student responds to questions from teammates. "Why would it be that accomplishment?" "Have you ever done anything like that?" When the time limit is up, students say "Thank you," and the interviewed student sits down. The next student stands up and is interviewed by teammates. The team interview is over when all students have been interviewed.

Team Interview is a great way to have students share information and feel mutually supported. Every student gets to be in the spotlight with their teammates' full attention.

1 Teacher Announces a Topic

Announce a topic on which students are to interview each other. *"Find out what your teammate did over the weekend."*

2 Students Interview First Teammate

One student stands up. He or she is the first interviewee. Teammates can ask the teammate any question they want.

③ Remaining Teammates Interviewed

After the first student is interviewed, he or she sits down. The student to the left stands up and becomes the interviewee. The team interview continues until all students have been interviewed.

H i n t s

★ **Pre-Made Questions.** Announce the topic and have the class or teams generate interesting questions before the interview begins.

★ **Timekeeper.** Assign the role of timekeeper. The timekeeper thanks each interviewee at the end of his or her allotted time. The teacher may be the timekeeper announcing time to the class.

★ **Open-ended Questions.** Teach and practice with students how to ask open-ended questions to promote elaboration and avoid short answers.

★ **Right to Pass.** The interviewee has the right to pass on any question he or she does not feel comfortable answering. He or she just says "pass" and the team asks the next question. Instead of passing, students may answer questions they wish they were asked.

Two Questions

Rather than using a time limit, use a question limit. Each student must ask the interviewee two questions before he or she may sit down. This equalizes participation among interviewers.

RoundRobin Q's

Another way to equalize participation is to have each teammate ask their questions in RoundRobin fashion (taking turns).

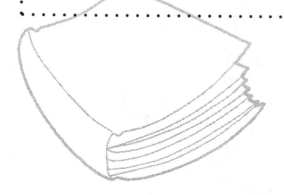

P r i n c i p l e s

The knowledge of the interviewee becomes the knowledge of the interviewers.

Each student is accountable for asking questions when they are the interviewer, and answering when they are interviewing.

Every student is interviewed. RoundRobin interview questions ensures equality among interviewers.

Interviewing is going on in every team in the class simultaneously. At least a quarter of the class is actively involved at once.

Team Interview

Kagans: *Cooperative Learning Structures for Teambuilding*©
Kagan Cooperative Learning • 1(800) WEE CO-OP

Question 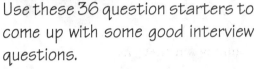 Starters

1. What is...

2. Where/when did...

3. Which is...

4. Who is...

5. What is...

6. How is...

7. What did...

8. Where/when did...

9. Which did...

10. Who did...

11. Why did...

12. How did...

13. What can...

14. Where/when can...

15. Which can...

16. Who can...

17. Why can...

18. How can...

19. What would...

Use these 36 question starters to come up with some good interview questions.

20. When/where would...

21. Which would...

22. Who would...

23. Why would...

24. How would...

25. What will...

26. Where/when will...

27. Which will

28. Who will...

29. Why will

30. How will...

31. What might...

32. Where/when might...

33. Which might...

34. Who might...

35. Why might...

36. How might..

Question starters from Chuck Wiederhold's
Cooperative Learning and Higher Level Thinking

Team Interview 137

You're Rich and Famous

Fill in all the information about being rich and famous. Get ready to ask your teammates questions about being rich and famous and answer questions about yourself.

You're rich and famous for _____

_____

_____
_____
_____
_____
_____
_____
_____
_____
_____
_____
_____

Bedroom Door Hanger

Make a sign to hang on your bedroom door. Think about words that describe you. Add a picture or pictures to decorate your door hanger. When you are done, cut it out. Get ready to ask your teammates questions about their door hangers and be prepared to answer questions about your door hanger.

Sample

A Few of My Favorite Things

Fill in your favorites. Get ready to ask your team-mates questions about their favorites and answer questions about your favorites.

Food _____

Drink _____

Color _____

Book _____

Subject _____

Sport _____

Athlete _____

Actor _____

TV Show _____

Hobby _____

Movie _____

Restaurant _____

Ice Cream _____

Flower _____

Animal _____

Band _____

Radio Station _____

The Perfect Vacation

Vacation time is here! Fill in all the information about your perfect vacation. Get ready to ask your teammates questions about their perfect vacation and answer questions about your perfect vacation.

For vacation I'd go _____

_____

I'd have to pack _____

_____

_____

Some things I'd like to do on vacation _____

_____

_____

_____

_____

_____

_____

You can expect me back _____

_____

_____

_____

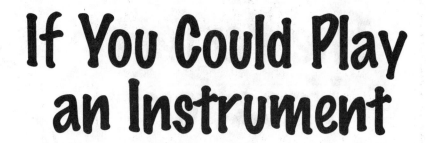

If You Could Play an Instrument

Have everyone pick an instrument. In turn teammates ask each other what instrument they would play, why they chose that instrument, where they would play it...

Your Special Someone

Have everyone think about a special someone. In turn teammates ask each other questions about their special someone like: Who is your special someone? Where did you meet? What do you do together? How old is he or she?

What Am I?

One student on the team selects something in the room. Teammates try to guess what it is. The student who selected the item says, "Too large," if teammates guess something too large and, "Too small," if teammates guess something too small. Teammates record their guesses on the sheet below. When teammates guess what the item is, they write it in the "Correct Guess" column and it is someone else's turn to pick an item in the room.

Too Small	Correct Guess	Too Large
2. chalk		1. desk
3. eraser		4. chair
5. book	6. globe	

Too Small	Correct Guess	Too Large

Team Projects

Teammates work cooperatively, each making an important contribution to the team project.

Team Projects can take an infinite number of forms. The procedure is really simple. The teacher announces the project or challenge, "Weather report predicts a heavy rainstorm. Build a team shelter out of newspapers and masking tape strong enough to keep your whole team warm and dry through the storm." Students work together to accomplish the team project.

Team Projects provides the opportunity for great student autonomy. Teammates feel a sense of mutual support and belonging when they are involved in cooperative projects working toward a common goal, especially when the project establishes a team identity.

Incorporating the basic principles of cooperative learning into Team Projects increases the likelihood of success. Team projects vary widely in both the process and the product. See Hints for some helpful guidelines.

2 Teams Complete Project

Students work cooperatively to do the team project.

1 Teacher Announces Project

Announce the team project, describing what the teams are to do and how they are to work together to accomplish the team project.

Hints for Team Projects

Team Projects can take many forms. With no structure, they can be chaos. Two easy ways to provide structure and ensure a successful team project are to: 1) Assign Roles, and 2) Limit the Resources.

Assign Roles

Roles are jobs for students. Assigning roles helps manage the social interaction among students. There are many roles from which to choose. Pick out the four most helpful roles for the project. Each role describes, "Things to Do" and "Things to Say." Role cards are helpful for students to remember their roles and what to say. Role cards are available for purchase, or you can make your own. If you make your own, have students brainstorm ideas for, "Things to Say."

front

Gatekeeper

back

Gatekeeper

Things To Say:
1. "Do you agree Susan?"

2. "Pete, what do you think?"

Things To Do:
Make sure everyone participates.

12 Social Roles

- Checker
- Cheerleader
- Coach
- Encourager
- Gatekeeper
- Materials Monitor
- Praiser
- Question Commander
- Quiet Captain
- Recorder
- Reflector
- Taskmaster

Limit the Resources

Without limits on resources, students are not interdependent and may work alone. Before starting the Team Project, write the "Materials" and "Who Touches" each material on the board.

Team Project

Materials	Who Touches
• 1 Large White Paper	All May Touch
• 8 Crayons	2 Colors Each
• 2 Scissors	Person 1 and 4
• 2 Glue Sticks	Person 2 and 3

Team Name

The Kool Kats

When a team is first formed, the team comes up with a team name. To come up with a team name, there are two rules: 1. Everyone must have a say in the name; 2) Everyone must agree on the team name.

Team names can be based on things that teammates have in common or the name can celebrate their differences. Have teams share their name with the class.

Team Handshake and Cheer

Have teams come up with a handshake and a cheer. There are two rules:
1) Everyone's hand must touch at some point in the handshake; 2) When they let go, the team makes a sound or shouts a word or phrase. The handshake and cheer can somehow symbolize the team name.

Teams can use their handshake and cheer to greet each other and celebrate success throughout their time together.

Team Logo or Banner

The Kool Kats

Have teams come up with a team logo or a team banner. The logo or the banner can include graphics, pictures, magazine clippings, text, team colors. The logo is usually made on an 8.5" x 11" sheet of paper; the banner can be done on large butcher or chart paper. Everyone must be involved in creating the team logo or banner. Have teams share their logo or banner with the class.

Team Hats

Laurie

Kool Kat

Teams are given painter's hats or assorted materials to make hats. They decide how their team hats are to look and then create and decorate their hats. The hats don't have to be identical, but something distinguishes them from the hats of another team. The hats may be based on the team name, but don't have to be. Teams can wear their thinking team hats when they work together on a project. Teams share their hats with the class.

T-Shirt Poster

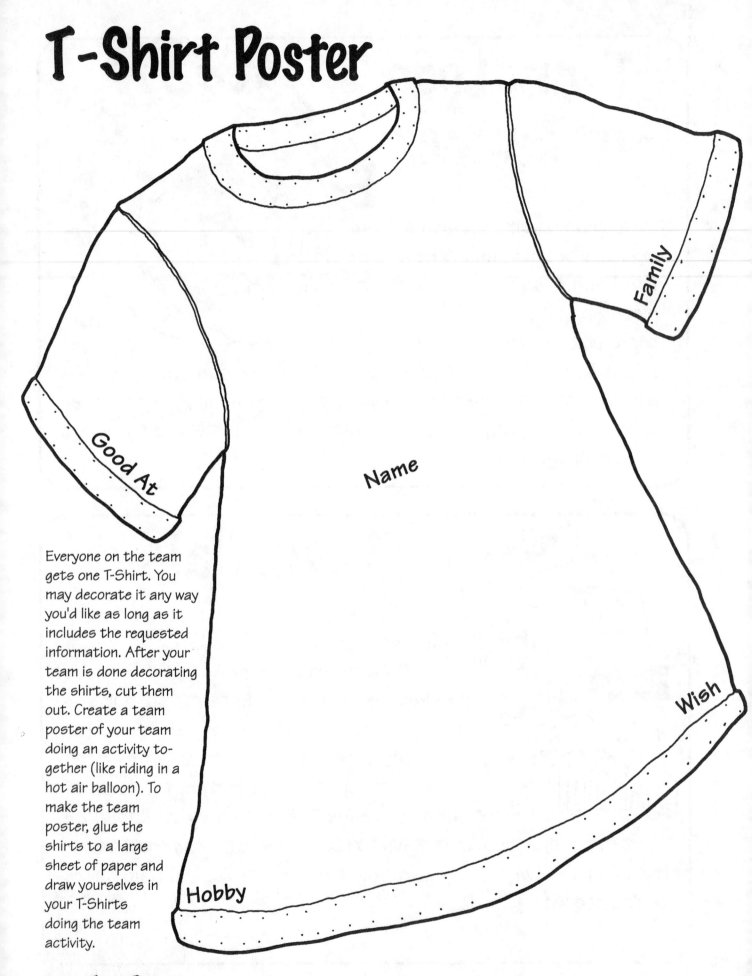

Family

Good At

Name

Wish

Everyone on the team gets one T-Shirt. You may decorate it any way you'd like as long as it includes the requested information. After your team is done decorating the shirts, cut them out. Create a team poster of your team doing an activity together (like riding in a hot air balloon). To make the team poster, glue the shirts to a large sheet of paper and draw yourselves in your T-Shirts doing the team activity.

Hobby

Team Caps

Everyone on the team gets one cap. Write your name on the cap. Decide whether you want to decorate your caps the same or want to make each one unique. After decorating your caps, cut them out. Paste your team's caps on a large sheet of paper. Write and decorate your team name across the top.

Team Green

Team Shields

Everyone on the team gets one shield. Fill in the information and decorate it however you please. Glue all your team shields on a poster and put your team name on the poster.

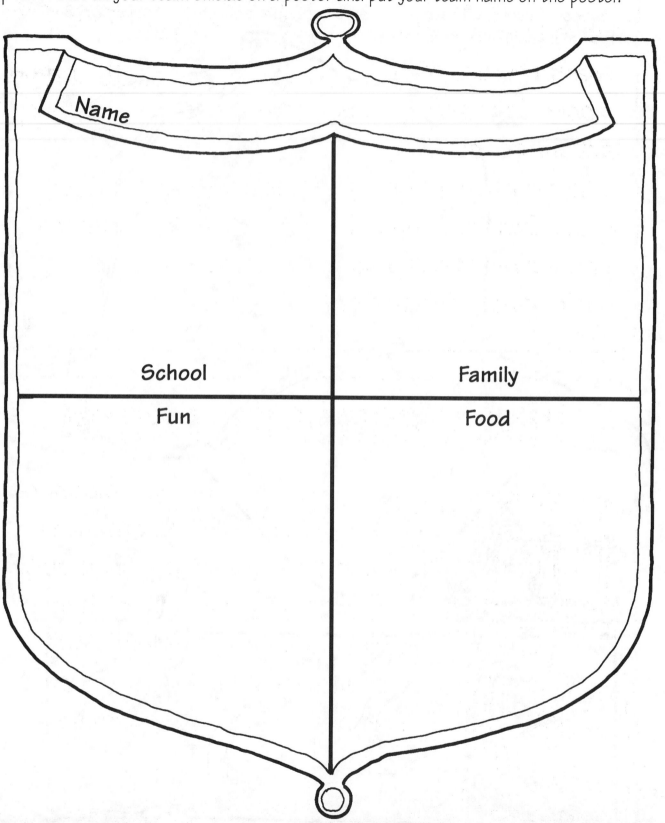

Team Tower

Have teams make a team tower out of blocks, legos, or common art materials like construction paper, glue, tape, crayons, paper clips. Everyone must be involved in the planning and building of the tower. Have teams share their tower with the class.

Pipe Cleaner Invention

Give each team 4 pipe cleaners per student. The team must plan their invention, then build it. Students can only touch their own pipe cleaners. Randomly call one student on the team to present the invention to the class.

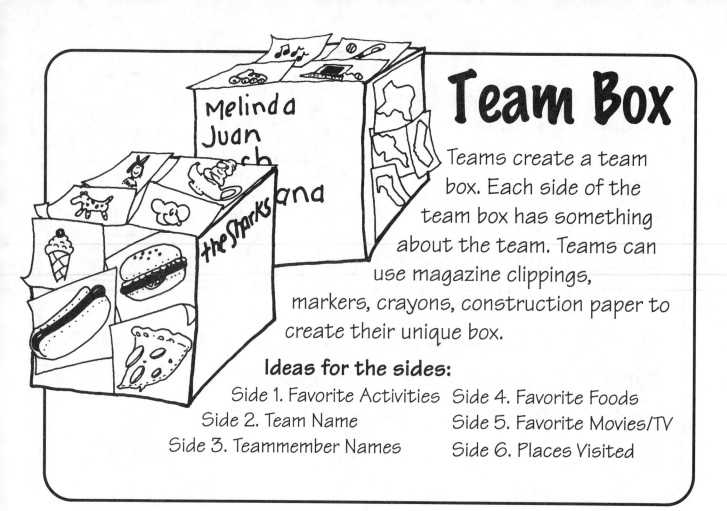

Team Box

Teams create a team box. Each side of the team box has something about the team. Teams can use magazine clippings, markers, crayons, construction paper to create their unique box.

Ideas for the sides:

Side 1. Favorite Activities
Side 2. Team Name
Side 3. Teammember Names

Side 4. Favorite Foods
Side 5. Favorite Movies/TV
Side 6. Places Visited

Silhouettes

The Book Sharks

Point an overhead projector at a wall. Teams tape construction paper to the wall. One teammate stands near the wall and another teammate traces the silhouette. A different color piece of construction paper is taped to the wall and the next teammate is traced. Students cut out their silhouettes. The silhouettes are glued on top of each other to make the team silhouette. Everyone gets a chance to trace, cut and glue.

Teams Solve a Puzzle

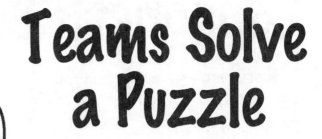

Teams work together on a puzzle. The puzzle can be a jigsaw puzzle, 3D puzzle, crossword puzzle, word search, word problem, riddle, maze... Have teams reflect on how equal the participation was and discuss how they could equalize participation. Give teams a second similar puzzle to try, then reflect on their participation.

Write How to...

Teams write instructions for doing a specific task. The idea is to make the instructions so concise that a Martian could land on earth and perform the task with just the instructions. It is helpful for students to act out the steps as they are being written and to revise.

How to... Ideas:
- How to eat a plate of spaghetti.
- How to make a peanut butter and jelly sandwich.
- How to juggle.
- How to solve a math problem.
- How to ride a bicycle.
- How to drive a car.
- How to swim.
- How to read a clock.

Spaghetti Space Station

Each student gets 4 pieces of raw spaghetti and 4 gumdrops. The team's job is to build a spaghetti space station. Students can only touch their own spaghetti and gumdrops.

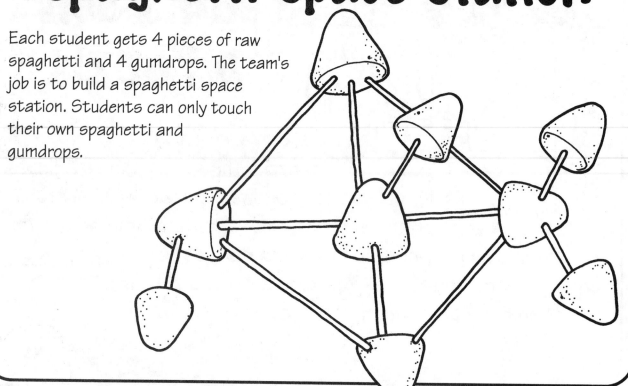

Team Mobile

Teams create a mobile to hang over their desks. For each team, make one, two or four copies of the sheet at right depending on how large you'd like the mobiles. To make the mobile, teams fill in information for each picture (see ideas below), color the pieces, cut them out, tape or glue them front to back then suspend them with string or yarn from a clothes hanger. Teams can cover the wire hanger with their team name decorated on construction paper.

The Daring Dolphins

Category Ideas:
- Car - Places I've visited, places I'd like to go
- Plate - Favorite food, restaurant, dessert
- TV - Favorite TV show, movie, video
- Book - Favorite book, story, poem
- Boat - Favorite free-time activity

Pieces for Team Mobile

Cut out these pieces for your team mobile.

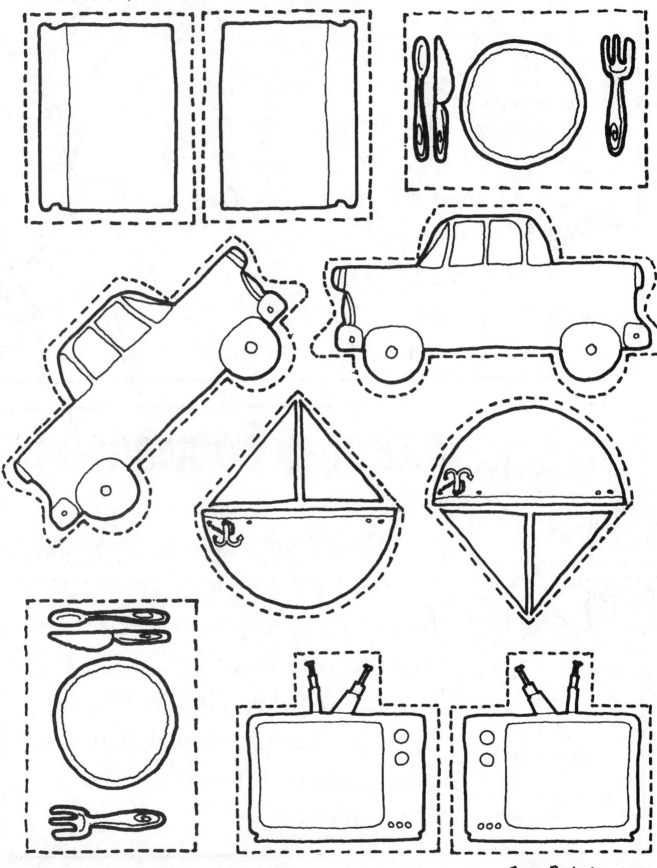

Mirror Walk

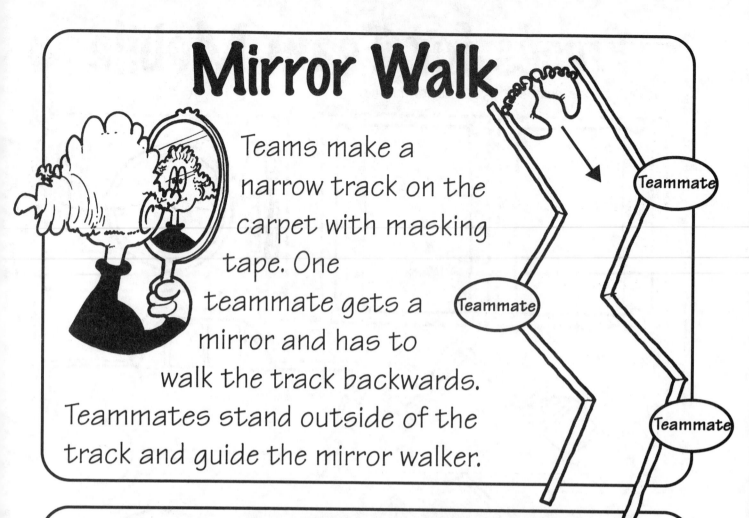

Teams make a narrow track on the carpet with masking tape. One teammate gets a mirror and has to walk the track backwards. Teammates stand outside of the track and guide the mirror walker.

Teammate

Teammate

Teammate

Balloon Bounce

A team forms a circle by joining hands. They bounce a balloon in the air without letting go of their hands. When they get good, they try two and three balloons at once. If a balloon lands on the ground, they must pick it up and continue without letting go of their hands.

Blindfolded

Teammates form pairs. One partner is blindfolded or closes his or her eyes. The other is the tour guide. The tour guide leads the blindfolded partner around the room and describes items in the room by placing his or her partners hands on the item. Pairs switch roles.

The Worm

Teammates stand in a line with their hands on the hips of the person in front of them. The leader has his or her eyes open and the rest of the teammates have their eyes closed. The leader leads teammates around the room and makes sure no one bumps into anything. Everyone takes a turn at being the leader.

Team Statements

Teams devise a synergistic team statement based on each student's contribution. Teams share their statements with the class or another team.

The teacher announces to the class a topic on which each team is to create a statement. For instance, the teacher may say, "A team is..." Students think about the statements they would make and then form pairs within their teams to discuss the topic. After the pair discussion, independently students write down their own statement. After everyone has written a statement, the team reunites. Each student in turn shares his or her statement with the team. When everyone has shared a statement, the team discusses the individual statements and tries to uncover the essence of each statement. The team then tries to capture the essence of all statements in one team statement. Once the team has achieved consensus on a team statement, each team shares their statement with the class or another team.

Team statements are a great way to unleash the power of team synergy. Teams draw from the strengths of individual statements to capture the underlying essence of the topic in one team statement.

1 **Think Time**

Announce the topic. Give students a good 20 seconds of think time before having students discuss the topic in pairs.

2 **Pairs Discuss**

In pairs, students discuss the topic.

3 **Individuals Write**

Each student writes his or her own statement on a sheet of paper.

Team Statement

6 Teams Share

When every team has a statement, each team shares their statements with the class or with another team.

4 RoundRobin

In turn, each student shares their statement with the team. Tell students to suspend discussing the individual statements until every one has a chance to read his or her statement to the team.

5 Team Statement

After each student has read his or her statement to the team, the team discusses the individual statements. The team comes up with one statement which best captures the essence of what all the individuals expressed in their individual statements.

Hints

★ **Describe the Steps.** Team Statements involves many steps. To give students the big picture, briefly outline the steps before starting.

★ **Think Time.** Give students at least 20 seconds to think about the topic before they discuss it with a partner. Think time promotes deeper level thinking and enriches the discussion.

★ **Question Time.** Teams can ask questions about each others' statements.

★ **Three Blind Men.** Remind students of the parable of the three blind men and the elephant. Each of us has a part of the truth. All of us are smarter than any one of us.

★ **Stringing Beads.** Remind students that a team statement is not like stringing beads—it is not creating one long run-on sentence from the individual sentences. Often the best team statement is shorter than any of the individual statements—it catches the underlying essence from which the individual sentences sprung.

★ **Blackboard Share.** To simultaneously share statements, have teams write or post their statements on the chalkboard or have each team record their statement in a class book on the topic.

★ **Sponge Activity.** Since teams may finish at different rates, use a sponge activity for teams which complete their statement. Teams can illustrate their statement.

Pair Statements

Have students come up with a statement in pairs: 1) Think Time - Give students time to think about what they are going to write before they write; 2) Individuals Write - Students write their statements individually; 3) RallyRobin - Partners take turns reading their statement; 4) Pair Statement - Pair works together to come up with a pair statement; 5) Pairs Share - Pairs share their statement with another pair or with the class.

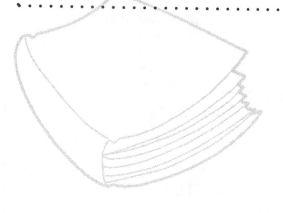

Principles

P POSITIVE INTERDEPENDENCE

The ideas of each individual contribute to the team's statement.

I INDIVIDUAL ACCOUNTABILITY

Every student is accountable to the team for coming up with an individual statement.

E EQUAL PARTICIPATION

Each student comes up with and shares his or her statement with the team.

S SIMULTANEOUS INTERACTION

All teams are simultaneously working on their statements.

Team Statements

A Hero is...

Write your final team statement neatly and in large text to post or share with the class.

The Hardest Part of Growing Up is...

Write your final team statement neatly and in large text to post or share with the class.

Our Team is Special because...

Write your final team statement neatly and in large text to post or share with the class.

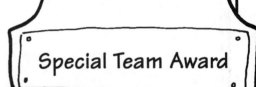

Special Team Award

A Good Teammate is...

Write your final team statement neatly and in large text to post or share with the class.

Listening is Important because...

Mark Twain said, "If we were supposed to talk more than we listen, we would have two mouths and one ear." Come up with a team statement why listening is important. Write your final team statement neatly and in large text to post or share with the class.

School Would be Better if...

Write your final team statement neatly and in large text to post or share with the class.

Working Together is Important because ...

Write your final team statement neatly and in large text to post or share with the class.

Three-Step Interview

Students become interviewers and reporters. Students interview their partner and then report what they learned about their teammate to the rest of the team.

The teacher presents a topic on which students interview each other. "Find out what your partner did for summer vacation." Students form pairs within their teams. In pairs, Student A interviews Student B for one minute (or whatever time limit is set). Student B then interviews Student A. Pairs join together to form a team of four. In teams, each student in turn shares with teammates what he or she learned from his or her partner. The interview is done when each teammate has had a chance to report to the team what he or she learned from his or her teammate.

Three-Step Interview is a great way to have students share information (especially personal information) in a nonthreatening way. Students open up as a teammate gives them full, undivided attention. Students listen well because they know they will be accountable to share the information with the team.

1 A's Interview B's

The teacher announces a topic, then students in pairs begin the interview. In each pair, Student A's are the interviewers. It is their job to listen to Student B for the time allotted and prepare to share the information with the team.

2 B's Interview A's

Students switch roles. Students B's become the interviewers and Student A's the interviewees.

3 RoundRobin

Pairs join together to form a team of four. Each student in turn shares with the team what he or she learned from his or her partner.

★ **Listen Carefully.** Tell the class to listen carefully to their partners because they will have to share the information they learn with the team. If students know beforehand that they will need to share the information, they listen more intently.

★ **Model Interviewing Skills.** Model what a good interviewer does and says. A good interviewer appears interested, maintains contact and is sure to say, "Thank you for sharing that information. I'll do my best to present it as accurately as possible."

★ **Take Notes.** It may help some students to take notes about their partner. They may refer to their notes as they report about their partner.

★ **The Right to Correct.** Only if a partner is sharing incorrect information with the team, can the student being reported about share about himself. Otherwise, teammates are responsible for sharing what their partner said.

★ **Use a Timekeeper.** One student on the team is the timekeeper. It is the task of the timekeeper to make sure students interview each other for the proper amount of time. The teacher may be the timekeeper.

H i n t s

New Pair Share

After having students share with the team, have them form a pair with another student outside of the team and share the information with the new partner.

Four-Step Interview

Younger children have a hard time remembering what their partners have told them, especially if they are interviewed about themselves before they have a chance to share what they have just heard. To solve this problem, use Four-Step Interview. Step 1. In pairs, one student interviews the other. Step 2. The two interviewers tell the team what they just learned. Step 3. Pairs reform and the interviewer becomes the interviewee. Step 4. The two new interviewers share with the team what they just learned.

Six-Step Interview

This is a variation for shy, limited English proficient students and primary students who may find it difficult to talk to three other students. Six-Step allows students to talk to only one student at a time. Step 1. In pairs, one student interviews the other. Step 2. Pairs reverse roles of interviewer and interviewee. Step 3. Students form a new pair and one shares what they just leaned about their partner. Step 4. In the same pair, the other student shares about his or her old partner. Step 5. Still in the same pair, one partner interviews the other. Step 6. Students reverse roles and interviewee becomes the interviewer. In short, Six-Step Interview goes like this: Interview, Interview, Share, Share, Interview, Interview.

Three-Pair-Share

Another pair interview format, excellent for primary and early language learners, is a Three-Pair-Share. Students simply interview and are interviewed by one teammate. Students do the interview three times, once with each teammate.

Microphone Interview

To make the interview more fun and focused for younger students, have students use phony microphones (paper towel roll and tennis ball) to interview their partner.

Principles

Students depend on each other to learn about their teammates.

Students are accountable to their partner for listening and accountable to the team for sharing correct information.

All students interview, are interviewed and share information with the team.

Students simultaneously interview in pairs and share in teams.

Three-Step Interview

Kagans: *Cooperative Learning Structures for Teambuilding*©
Kagan Cooperative Learning • 1 (800) WEE CO-OP

Outlaw Interview

Sheriff in town is looking for your outlaw partner. Interview your partner, and get all the information you can to help the sheriff. Draw a picture of your partner. Share the information and your picture of your outlaw partner with the team.

Favorite Eating Spot

Best Found with

WANTED

Age

Hangout

Other info: _____

_____

_____

_____

_____

On the Front Page

You're writing an article for the Gazette's front page featuring what your teammate did for the weekend. Interview your teammate, then write a headline and draw a picture. Share with the team books, movies and sports your teammate enjoys.

the **Gazette**

ISSUE NO. _____   PRICE _____

HEADLINE _____

PICTURE

📖 Books I've Enjoyed    🎥 Movies I've Enjoyed    ⚾ Sports I've Enjoyed

Buy a Quality

You have $100 to buy qualities of a new teammate. You can only spend $100, so spend it wisely. Circle your selections.

Responsible $50

Fun $25

Trusting $50

Creative $25

Friendly $50

Kind $50

Happy $25

Dependable $50

Athletic $50

Honest $25

Patient $25

Perfect $200

Write a paragraph explaining what you spent your money on and why. Interview your partner about what he or she spent his or her money on and why. Be ready to share your partner's answer with the team.

_____

_____

_____

_____

_____

_____

_____

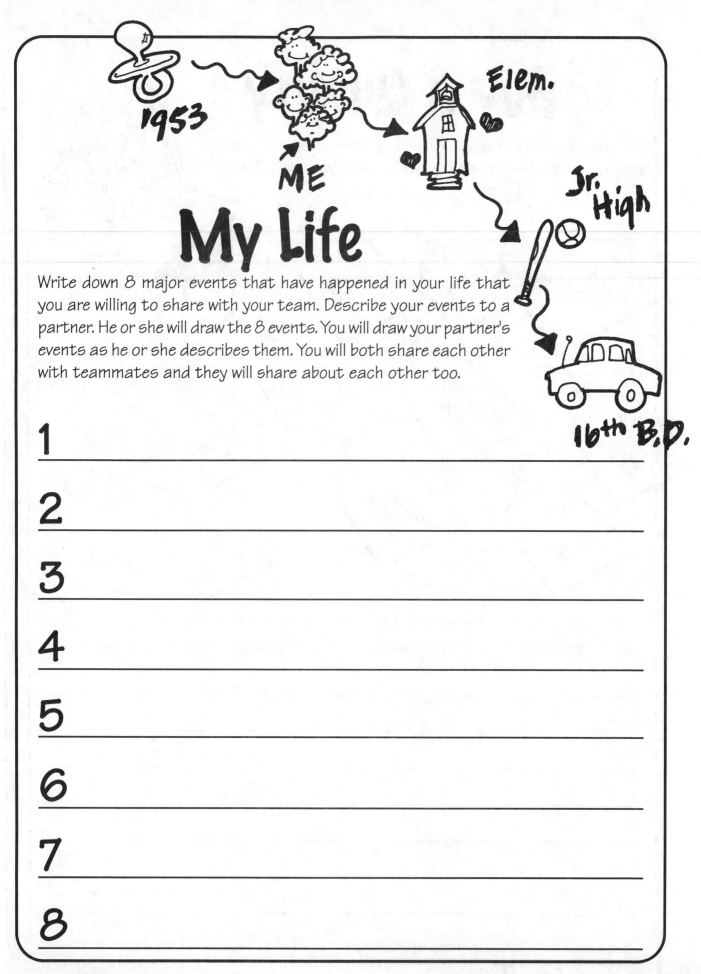

My Life

1953

ME

Elem.

Jr. High

16th B.D.

Write down 8 major events that have happened in your life that you are willing to share with your team. Describe your events to a partner. He or she will draw the 8 events. You will draw your partner's events as he or she describes them. You will both share each other with teammates and they will share about each other too.

1 _____

2 _____

3 _____

4 _____

5 _____

6 _____

7 _____

8 _____

My Partner's Life

In the space below, draw the events of your partner's life as he or she describes them to you. Draw them so you can share the events with teammates.

Partner's Name

Qualities of a Friend

Rank the qualities of a friend that are important to you with stars. Pick the top three qualities and share with a partner why you chose those qualities. Listen to why your partner chose the three he or she did and share your partner's answer with your team.

> ★ ★ ★ = Most important qualities
> ★ ★ = Important qualities
> ★ = Not that important

____affectionate	____fun	____popular
____appreciative	____funny	____positive
____attractive	____generous	____respectful
____athletic	____giving	____responsible
____available	____good listener	____sharing
____caring	____happy	____sincere
____common interests	____helpful	____smart
____common personality	____honest	____stable
	____keeps secrets	____strong
____common values	____kind	____supportive
____daring	____loving	____sympathetic
____dependable	____loyal	____talented
____energetic	____mature	____talkative
____exciting	____motivational	____thoughtful
____friendly	____outgoing	____trustworthy
____forgiving	____patient	____understanding
	____playful	____unpredictable

Character Map

In pairs, make a character map for your partner as he or she describes himself or herself. To make a character map, write your partner's name in the center and an adjective describing your partner coming off each line. For each adjective, give evidence and the results (see example). Share your partner's character map with your team.

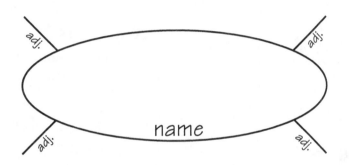

name

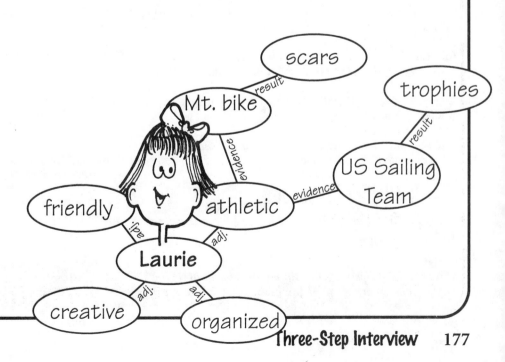

a selected Resource List

Classbuilding and Teambuilding

Books of Classbuilding and Teambuilding activities

Craigen, Jim & Ward, Chris. *What's This Got to do with Anything? A Collection of Group/Class Builders and Energizers.* Canada: VISUTronX, 1996.

Gibbs, Jeanne. *Tribes.* Santa Rosa, CA: Center Source Publications, 1987.

Kagan, Miguel, Robertson, Laurie & Kagan, Spencer. *Cooperative Learning Structures for Classbuilding.* San Clemente, CA: Kagan Cooperative Learning, 1995.

Scearce, Carol. *100 Ways to Build Teams.* Arlington Heights, IL: IRI Skylight, 1992.

Shaw, Vanston. *Communitybuilding in the Classroom.* San Juan Capistrano, CA: Kagan Cooperative Learning, 1994.

Williams, R. Bruce. *More than 50 Ways to Build Team Consensus.* Palatine, IL: IRI Skylight, 1993.

Cooperative Learning

Books that promote Teambuilding through the use of cooperative learning

Cohen, Elizabeth G. *Designing Groupwork: Strategies for the Heterogeneous Classroom.* New York, NY: Teachers College Press, 1994.

Johnson D.W. et al. *Circles of Learning: Cooperation in the Classroom.* Edina, MN: Interaction Book Company, 1993.

Kagan, Spencer. *Cooperative Learning.* San Clemente, CA: Kagan Cooperative Learning, 1994.

McCabe, M.E. & Rhoades, J. *The Nurturing Classroom.* Sacramento, CA: ITA Publications, 1990.

The Inclusive Classroom

Books that promote Teambuilding by creating an inclusive classroom

Duvall, Lynn. *Respecting Our Differences: A Guide to Getting Along in a Changing World.* Minneapolis, MN: Free Spirit Press, 1994.

Moorman, C. & Dishon, D. *Our Classroom: We Can Learn Together.* Portage, MI: Personal Power Press, 1983.

Schniedewind, N. & Davidson, E. *Open Minds to Equality.* Englewood Cliffs, NJ: Prentice-Hall, 1983.

Social Skills

Books that promote Teambuilding through the teaching of social skills

Bellanca, James. *Building a Caring, Cooperative Classroom.* Palatine, IL: Skylight Publishing, 1991.

Cartledge, G & Milburn, J.F., Eds. *Teaching Social Skills to Children.* Elmsford, NY: Pergamon Press, 1986.

Cowan, D. et al. *Teaching the Skills of Conflict Resolution.* Spring Valley, CA: Innerchoice Publishing, 1992.

Drew, Naomi. *Learning the Skills of Peacemaking.* Rolling Hills Estates, CA: Jalmar Press, 1987.

Feshbach, N. et al. *Learning To Care.* Glenview, IL: Scott Foresman & Company, 1983.

Goldstein, Arnold P. *The Prepare Curriculum: Teaching Prosocial Competencies.* Champaign, IL: Research Press, 1988.

Johnson, D. & Johnson, R. *Teaching Children To Be Peace-makers.* Edina, MN: Interaction Book Company, 1991.

Kreidler, William J. *Elementary Perspectives: Teaching Concepts of Peace & Conflict.* Cambridge, MA: Educators for Social Responsibility, 1990.

Kreidler, William J. *Conflict Resolution in the Middle School.* Cambridge, MA: Educators for Social Responsibility, 1994.

Levin, Diane E. *Teaching Young Children in Violent Times: Building a Peaceable Classroom.* Cambridge, MA: Educators for Social Responsibility, 1994

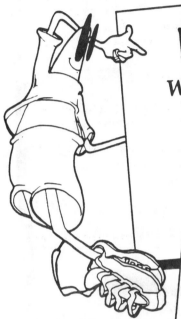